Summer Reading: Closing the Rich/Poor Achievement Gap
RICHARD L. ALLINGTON & ANNE MCGILL-FRANZEN, EDS.

Real World Writing for Secondary Students:
Teaching the College Admission Essay and Other
Gate-Openers for Higher Education
JESSICA SINGER EARLY & MEREDITH DeCOSTA

Teaching Vocabulary to English Language Learners
MICHAEL F. GRAVES, DIANE AUGUST,
& JEANNETTE MANCILLA-MARTINEZ

Literacy for a Better World:
The Promise of Teaching in Diverse Schools
LAURA SCHNEIDER VANDERPLOEG

Socially Responsible Literacy:
Teaching Adolescents for Purpose and Power
PAULA M. SELVESTER & DEBORAH G. SUMMERS

Learning from Culturally and Linguistically
Diverse Classrooms: Using Inquiry to Inform Practice
JOAN C. FINGON & SHARON H. ULANOFF, EDS.

Bridging Literacy and Equity
ALTHIER M. LAZAR, PATRICIA A. EDWARDS, &
GWENDOLYN THOMPSON MCMILLON

"Trust Me! I Can Read"
SALLY LAMPING & DEAN WOODRING BLASE

Reading Girls
HADAR DUBOWSKY MA'AYAN

Reading Time
CATHERINE COMPTON-LILLY

A Call to Creativity
LUKE REYNOLDS

Literacy and Justice Through Photography
WENDY EWALD, KATHERINE HYDE, & LISA LORD

The Successful High School Writing Center
DAWN FELS & JENNIFER WELLS, EDS.

Interrupting Hate
MOLLIE V. BLACKBURN

Playing Their Way into Literacies
KAREN E. WOHLWEND

Teaching Literacy for Love and Wisdom
JEFFREY D. WILHELM & BRUCE NOVAK

Overtested
JESSICA ZACHER PANDYA

Restructuring Schools for Linguistic Diversity, Second Edition
OFELIA B. MIRAMONTES, ADEL NADEAU, & NANCY L. COMMINS

Words Were All We Had
MARÍA DE LA LUZ REYES, ED.

Urban Literacies
VALERIE KINLOCH, ED.

Bedtime Stories and Book Reports
CATHERINE COMPTON-LILLY & STUART GREENE, EDS.

Envisioning Knowledge
JUDITH A. LANGER

Envisioning Literature, Second Edition
JUDITH A. LANGER

Writing Assessment and the Revolution in
Digital Texts and Technologies
MICHAEL R. NEAL

Artifactual Literacies
KATE PAHL & JENNIFER ROWSELL

Educating Emergent Bilinguals
OFELIA GARCÍA & JO ANNE KLEIFGEN

(Re)Imagining Content-Area Literacy Instruction
RONI JO DRAPER, ED.

Change Is Gonna Come
PATRICIA A. EDWARDS, GWENDOLYN THOMPSON MCMILLON, &
JENNIFER D. TURNER

When Commas Meet Kryptonite
MICHAEL BITZ

Literacy Tools in the Classroom
RICHARD BEACH, GERALD CAMPANO, BRIAN EDMISTON,
& MELISSA BORGMANN

Harlem on Our Minds
VALERIE KINLOCH

Teaching the New Writing
ANNE HERRINGTON, KEVIN HODGSON, & CHARLES MORAN, EDS.

Critical Encounters in High School English, Second Edition
DEBORAH APPLEMAN

Children, Language, and Literacy
CELIA GENISHI & ANNE HAAS DYSON

Children's Language
JUDITH WELLS LINDFORS

The Administration and Supervision of Reading Programs,
Fourth Edition
SHELLEY B. WEPNER & DOROTHY S. STRICKLAND, EDS.

"You Gotta BE the Book," Second Edition
JEFFREY D. W

No Quick Fix
RICHARD L. A

Children's Lite
BARBARA A.

Storytime
LARWRENCE R. SIPE

Effective Instruction for Struggling Readers, K–6
BARBARA M. TAYLOR & JAMES E. YSSELDYKE, EDS.

The Effective Literacy Coach
ADRIAN RODGERS & EMILY M. RODGERS

Writing in Rhythm
MAISHA T. FISHER

Reading the Media
RENEE HOBBS

teaching**media**/iteracy.com
RICHARD BEACH

(continued)

For volumes in the NCRLL Collection (edited by JoBeth Allen and Donna E. Alvermann) and the Practitioners Bookshelf Series (edited by Celia Genishi and Donna E. Alvermann), please visit www.tcpress.com.

What Was It Like?
LINDA J. RICE

Once Upon a Fact
CAROL BRENNAN JENKINS & ALICE EARLE

Research on Composition
PETER SMAGORINSKY, ED.

Critical Literacy/Critical Teaching
CHERYL DOZIER, PETER JOHNSTON, & REBECCA ROGERS

The Vocabulary Book
MICHAEL F. GRAVES

Building on Strength
ANA CELIA ZENTELLA, ED.

Powerful Magic
NINA MIKKELSEN

New Literacies in Action
WILLIAM KIST

Teaching English Today
BARRIE R.C. BARRELL ET AL., EDS.

Bridging the Literacy Achievement Gap, 4–12
DOROTHY S. STRICKLAND & DONNA E. ALVERMANN, EDS.

Crossing the Digital Divide
BARBARA MONROE

Out of This World
HOLLY VIRGINIA BLACKFORD

Critical Passages
KRISTIN DOMBEK & SCOTT HERNDON

Making Race Visible
STUART GREENE & DAWN ABT-PERKINS, EDS.

The Child as Critic, Fourth Edition
GLENNA SLOAN

Room for Talk
REBEKAH FASSLER

Give Them Poetry!
GLENNA SLOAN

The Brothers and Sisters Learn to Write
ANNE HAAS DYSON

"Just Playing the Part"
CHRISTOPHER WORTHMAN

The Testing Trap
GEORGE HILLOCKS, JR.

Reading Lives
DEBORAH HICKS

Inquiry Into Meaning
EDWARD CHITTENDEN & TERRY SALINGER, WITH ANNE M. BUSSIS

"Why Don't They Learn English?"
LUCY TSE

Conversational Borderlands
BETSY RYMES

Inquiry-Based English Instruction
RICHARD BEACH & JAMIE MYERS

The Best for Our Children
MARÍA DE LA LUZ REYES & JOHN J. HALCÓN, EDS.

Language Crossings
KAREN L. OGULNICK, ED.

What Counts as Literacy?
MARGARET GALLEGO & SANDRA HOLLINGSWORTH, EDS.

Beginning Reading and Writing
DOROTHY S. STRICKLAND & LESLEY M. MORROW, EDS.

Reading for Meaning
BARBARA M. TAYLOR, MICHAEL F. GRAVES,
& PAUL VAN DEN BROEK, EDS.

Young Adult Literature and the New Literary Theories
ANNA O. SOTER

Literacy Matters
ROBERT P. YAGELSKI

Children's Inquiry
JUDITH WELLS LINDFORS

Close to Home
JUAN C. GUERRA

Life at the Margins
JULIET MERRIFIELD ET AL.

Literacy for Life
HANNA ARLENE FINGERET & CASSANDRA DRENNON

The Book Club Connection
SUSAN I. MCMAHON & TAFFY E. RAPHAEL, EDS., ET AL.

Until We Are Strong Together
CAROLINE E. HELLER

Writing Superheroes
ANNE HAAS DYSON

Opening Dialogue
MARTIN NYSTRAND ET AL.

Just Girls
MARGARET J. FINDERS

The First R
MICHAEL F. GRAVES, PAUL VAN DEN BROEK, &
BARBARA M. TAYLOR, EDS.

Talking Their Way into Science
KAREN GALLAS

The Languages of Learning
KAREN GALLAS

Partners in Learning
CAROL LYONS, GAY SU PINNELL, & DIANE DEFORD

Social Worlds of Children Learning to Write
in an Urban Primary School
ANNE HAAS DYSON

Inside/Outside
MARILYN COCHRAN-SMITH & SUSAN L. LYTLE

Whole Language Plus
COURTNEY B. CAZDEN

Learning to Read
G. BRIAN THOMPSON & TOM NICHOLSON, EDS.

Engaged Reading
JOHN T. GUTHRIE & DONNA E. ALVERMANN

Summer Reading

Closing the Rich/Poor Reading Achievement Gap

EDITED BY

Richard L. Allington
Anne McGill-Franzen

Foreword by Gerald G. Duffy

Teachers College, Columbia University
New York and London

International Reading Association
Newark, DE

Published simultaneously by Teachers College Press, 1234 Amsterdam Avenue, New York, NY 10027 and the International Reading Association, 800 Barksdale Road, Newark, DE 19711.

Library of Congress Cataloging-in-Publication Data

Summer reading : closing the rich/poor reading achievement gap / edited by Richard L. Allington, Anne McGill-Franzen.
    p. cm.— (Language and literacy series)
  Includes bibliographical references and index.
  ISBN 978-0-8077-5374-3 (pbk.)
    1. Supplementary reading—United States. 2. Summer reading programs—United States. 3. Poor children—Books and reading—United States. 4. Reading—Remedial teaching—United States. I. Allington, Richard L. II. McGill-Franzen, Anne.
  LB1050.58S87 2012
  428.4—dc23   2012029632

ISBN 978-0-8077-5374-3 (paperback)

Printed on acid-free paper
Manufactured in the United States of America

20 19 18 17 16 15 14 13   8 7 6 5 4 3 2 1

Contents

Foreword

I am a voracious reader, thanks to my mother. My earliest memories are of her settling me in the children's room of the local library while she went upstairs to check out the popular novels she loved, and then reading those books, sometimes together on the front porch, sometimes curled up on the couch, and sometimes alone in bed before sleeping. Consequently, I learned early that books could transport me to magical places, take me out of my world and into others, and enlighten and enrich me in rewarding ways. In short, the volume of reading was not a problem for me and, as a result, reading is still an enduring joy of my life.

But I've learned in my 50 years of working in classrooms that not everyone is as lucky as I was. Many children have little opportunity to read for pleasure because, for various reasons, their mothers cannot do for them what my mother did for me. Of course, when this happens, schools are supposed to pick up the slack. And traditionally, they have done so, assuming responsibility for developing reading habits as well as reading skills. Sadly, however, that is seldom the case these days, because pleasure reading has been squeezed out of most classrooms by the pressures of accountability. The result is often children who have reading skills, but do not read.

Summer further exacerbates the problem. Children who get little opportunity to read during the school year get even less during the summer. Dick Allington and Anne McGill-Franzen, the editors of this volume, have long argued for making the volume of reading an integral part of classroom reading instruction, especially for struggling readers; more recently, they have also examined the issue of summer reading. This book is a summation of the work they and their coauthors have achieved. It describes the role reading volume plays in developing both avid and competent readers, and describes a variety of approaches to enhance summer reading opportunities for children. In sum, they make the case that summer reading is a potentially effective way to increase children's love of reading.

This is a particularly important book at this time when educational policy focuses almost exclusively on routine skills and standardized test scores. It provides a badly needed alternative perspective, and is a persuasive argument for providing all children with the gift my mother provided for me.

Gerald Duffy

Preface

WITH THIS BOOK we hope to raise the attention paid to summer reading loss. As noted in the opening chapter, summer reading loss accounts for roughly 80% of the reading achievement gap between more and less economically advantaged children (Alexander, Entwisle, & Olson, 2007). By the time both groups of children are nearing graduation from high school, the rich/poor reading achievement gap is 4 years wide, with children from low-income families performing at the same level as the middle-class children in 8th grade (NCES, 2010)! Because so many children of low-income families have dropped out of school before reaching 12th grade and only students remaining in school are assessed, the rich/poor reading achievement gap at age 17 is likely wider that the 4 years reported on the National Assessment of Educational Progress.

We cannot explain why policymakers continue to ignore summer reading loss given the focus on closing the reading achievement gap between rich and poor children that has guided federal policy since 1966 and the passage of the Elementary and Secondary Education Act, a major component of Lyndon Johnson's War on Poverty.

In Chapter 1, we attempt to provide a comprehensive review of what we know about summer reading loss. As we note, summer reading loss was identified as a problem worthy of consideration decades ago. It seems now that the lack of reading activity during the summer months that some students experience is the primary basis for explaining what has been observed repeatedly—poor children typically lose reading proficiency during the summers and more advantaged children show modest reading growth during the same period. It is also clear that children from low-income families have more restricted access to books than do more advantaged children. It isn't just children from low-income families who experience summer reading loss, but it is that population where that loss is nearly universal. Middle-class children who struggle with learning to read also experience summer reading loss, but far fewer middle-class children struggle with acquiring proficient reading behaviors than is the case with economically disadvantaged children. In fact, as we argue, any child who fails to engage in independent reading during the summer months will typically experience summer reading loss. In Chapter 2, James Lindsay presents a meta-analysis of research on children's access to print and their reading development. As he points out, experimental studies increasing children's access to print (books and magazines) produce positive effects on children's reading achievement, effects that are larger than the average effect sizes of all other educational interventions! Increasing children's access to print during the school year as well as during the summer had similar positive effects on reading achievement. This comprehensive meta-analysis provides strong evidence of the potential of various efforts to increase access to print and thereby enhance reading development.

In Chapter 3, we summarize the available research on stemming reading loss with a focus on studies that have increased low-income children's access to books during the summer months. What you may find surprising is just how consistently making books available to children from low-income families and to struggling readers enhances reading achievement during the summer months. In Chapter 4, Lunetta Williams discusses the power of self-selection when it comes to increasing children's access to books. She writes about the book choices and responses of a sample of Black children from largely low-income families. The children tell her why choice is such an important factor if we want to encourage voluntary reading, especially during the summer months.

Chapters 5 and 6 are written by practitioners from the field. In both chapters, you will find a heartening story of the power of providing children with self-selected books to read during the summer. In Chapter 5, Geri Melosh details a summer program that provides books to children who attend her north Florida elementary school. Using a donated pickup truck that now serves as a bookmobile, her students get their books for summer reading during weekly bookmobile visits to their rural homes. Melosh provides data demonstrating the success of this effort, success in terms of student performance on the state reading test. She also notes the affordability of this effort to close the rich/poor reading achievement gap. In Chapter 6, Lynn Bigelman describes her district's efforts to ensure that every child has books to read during the summer months. Finding funding to support the book purchases, partnering with local fast-food restaurants with free meals for summer readers, and a 1,000-minute summer reading challenge are each described, along with the effects of the summer reading initiative. After 4 years of success, Bigelman writes, she finds it difficult to believe that the district had never had a summer reading initiative. Given the community involvement and student successes, it is hard to imagine this initiative ever going away.

In Chapter 7, we attempt to bring closure to the book and to the topic of summer reading. We provide information on several other summer reading initiatives, including a school that converted an RV into a summer bookmobile and tutoring center and another where the reading specialist used her school telephone and its voicemail capacity to encourage children to call her number and leave a message about what they were reading over the summer. Several other research projects are discussed, with two comparing a reading intensive summer school to a traditional skills-based summer school, another examining the impact (or lack of impact) of a school-supplied summer reading list, and, finally, a report on a single summer books intervention with English Language Learners that did not seem to provide a positive effect beyond improved oral reading fluency but the authors argue that many of the books the children selected were too difficult given their reading levels and that the selection of the difficult books might have undermined broader gains.

Three issues—children's choice of books to read, the role of text complexity, and the reliable measurement of short-term academic gains—comprise the bulk of the remainder of Chapter 7. Each of these issues is important in any study of the effects of summer reading programs and each deserves more study.

For those who may be interested, the Appendix contains the report from the Coalition for Evidence-Based Policy on our summer books intervention. The Coalition finds our study provides "near top tier" evidence of an effective intervention for addressing the rich/poor reading achievement gap. The report notes that currently ours is the only study that meets the criteria for reliable research on the topic of an intervention designed to address summer reading setback. A second such study with children from a different location and perhaps from different grade levels is needed to have summer book distribution programs attain the Coalition's "top tier" ranking. We are currently seeking sponsorship to conduct such a study in the mountain communities of East Tennessee.

We hope that you will read the book and then act on what you have learned about the potential power of summer book distribution programs and the power of extensive reading summer school programs to change the future of poor children in your community and school. The children are waiting.

Richard L. Allington
Anne McGill-Franzen

REFERERNCES

Alexander, K. L., Entwisle, D. R., & Olson, L. S. (2007). Lasting consequences of the summer learning gap. *American Sociological Review, 72*(2), 167–180.

National Center for Educational Statistics. (2010). *NAEP 2009 reading: A report card for the nation and the states.* Washington, D.C.: Institute of Education Sciences, U.S. Department of Education.

CHAPTER 1

Summer Reading Loss

Richard L. Allington
Anne McGill-Franzen

ONCE AGAIN, policymakers are attempting to address the reading achievement gap that exists in educational performances of children from economically more- and less-advantaged families. Once again, the current preferred intervention designs seem targeted to the youngest students and to basic phonological skills development (Lyon, 2004). But we have been down this path—federal funding for code-emphasis early interventions—before, and there has been little evidence of much improvement in reading proficiency as a result of those efforts that dominated the 1970s, 1980s, 1990s, and the 2000s (Borman & D'Agostino, 1996; Donahue, Voelkl, Campbell, & Mazzeo, 1999; Gamse, Jacob, Horst, Boulay, & Unlu, 2009). Currently, the rich/poor reading achievement gap stands at 27 points in 4th grade, the same size the gap was in 2001 (Rampy, Dion, & Donahue, 2009). It is time to consider alternative directions in the campaign to close the rich/poor reading achievement gap.

This seems even more important today as we move into the era of the newly adopted Common Core State Standards (CCSS) for reading and language arts. Those standards emphasize a deeper form of understanding than simply asking readers to recall what they read. In addition, the CCSS emphasize increasing the complexity of the texts that students read at every grade level (Calkins, Ehrenworth, & Lehman, 2012). Much of what the CCSS require children to do has never actually been taught in schools in any systematic manner. In other words, the CCSS change the target when considering a child's proficiency as a reader. However, there is no reason to expect that children from low-income families will perform well on the assessments that will accompany the adoption of CCSS standards. It seems almost a given that with the CCSS, the achievement gap between low-income children and their economically better-off peers will remain just as large and just as intractable as it appears today.

Thirty years ago, researchers contrasting the reading achievement patterns in schools enrolling rich and poor students concluded:

> Our whole approach to equalizing educational opportunities and achievements may be misdirected. (Hayes & Grether, 1983, p. 66)

More recently, the authors of a similar study (Alexander, Entwisle, & Olsen, 2007) reached the same conclusion. In both of these large-scale research studies, the authors reported that that the achievement gap between rich and poor children grew dramatically across the elementary school years (from less than a year's difference upon entering kindergarten to almost 3 years' difference by the end of 6th grade). Both studies were designed such that achievement data for estimating student achievement at the beginning and end of each school year (September and June) were available. This information allowed the researchers to estimate both the reading growth during the school year and the accumulating impact of "summer reading loss."

Summer reading loss is that backsliding in reading development that can occur during the summer vacation periods, when children are not enrolled in school. The powerful negative impact of summer reading loss on poor children's longer-term reading achievement led both sets of researchers to argue that efforts targeted only at improving curriculum and instruction in high-poverty schools were unlikely to close the reading achievement gap between rich and poor children. In their view, in other words, much of the school reform effort aimed at improving the reading achievement of poor children has failed to focus professional attention on a critical factor implicated in producing the widening reading achievement gap—the poor child's summer reading loss.

THE RESEARCH ON SUMMER READING LOSS

Researchers have been reporting on the impact of summer reading loss for at least 30 years. For instance, in one of the earlier reports, Hayes and Grether (1983) studied fall-to-spring reading achievement data for students in 600 New York City elementary schools. The schools were first stratified into six categories by proportion of students receiving free or reduced-price lunches. They then compared the cumulative reading development of students in high- and low-poverty schools over time. This analysis demonstrated that a 7-month difference in reading achievement between the two groups of students at the beginning of grade 2 widened to a 2-year, 7-month difference at the end of grade 6.

However, their analyses of the achievement gains made during the academic year (fall-to-spring) illustrated that *students in both high-poverty and low-poverty schools made substantially similar gains when school was in session.* The effects of summer vacation (spring-to-fall comparisons) on reading achievement presented a very different pattern.

> The differential progress made during the four summers between 2nd and 6th grade accounts for upwards of 80 percent of the achievement difference between economically advantaged . . . and . . . ghetto schools. (Hayes & Grether, 1983, p. 64)

In other words, most of the large reading achievement gap found at grade 6 could be attributed to summer reading loss, along with the smaller initial achievement differences between the two groups of students when they began school.

More recently, Entwisle, Alexander, and Olson (1997) reported on their findings from the longitudinally designed Baltimore Beginning School Study, gathering achievement data from the beginning of grade 1 to the end of grade 6. In this case, the researchers randomly selected 790 students from 20 Baltimore elementary schools beginning in the fall of grade 1. Half the students were from high-poverty schools, half from economically more-advantaged schools. All students were administered a reading achievement test twice annually every fall and spring. This design also allowed comparisons of achievement patterns both during the school year and during summer vacation.

Once again, poor children had comparable achievement gains during the school year (fall-to-spring) across the period of study.

> At least through elementary school . . . the achievement levels of children from poor socioeconomic backgrounds increase on par with those from favored economic backgrounds when school is open. (Entwisle et. al, 1997, p. 152)

Nonetheless, at the end of grade 6, the achievement gap between rich and poor students had widened to almost a 3-year disparity. Again, an initial achievement discrepancy of less than a year had widened considerably, even though reading growth during the school year was comparable for both groups of students.

Most recently, Alexander, Entwisle, and Olson (2007) reported on the achievement differences between these same students at grade 9. Not surprisingly, they noted that summer reading loss among the children from low-income families continued to explain virtually all the differences in reading achievement between children from high- and low-income families. They wrote,

> We find that cumulative achievement gains over the first nine years of children's schooling mainly reflect school-year learning, whereas the high SES–low SES achievement gap at 9th grade mainly traces to differential summer learning over the elementary years. (p.167)

Similar evidence on the differential impact of summer vacation periods on more- and less-advantaged students' achievement has been available in the published scientific research literature for some time, and much of that research (13 empirical studies representing approximately 40,000 subjects) was subjected to a meta-analysis by Cooper, Nye, Charlton, Lindsay, and Greathouse (1996). In addition, Cooper et al. provided a narrative analysis of another two dozen studies that were available but that failed to provide adequate data for the meta-analytic procedures. Their summary findings echo the differential impact of summer vacation periods reported in the large-scale longitudinal studies reviewed above: Middle-class students' reading proficiency improved modestly in the summer while the proficiency of students from lower-income families declined.

According to Cooper et al. (1996), summer vacations created, on average, an annual achievement gap of about 3 months between rich and poor students, favoring, of course, the students from the more economically advantaged families. This 3-month annual gap accumulates to a year and a half achievement gap between the beginning of grade 1 and the end of grade 6 (over five summers). When this accumulating reading achievement gap is combined with an initial achievement gap (at the beginning of schooling), students from lower-income families often find themselves 2 or 3 years behind their more-advantaged peers as they head to middle school—even when they receive effective instruction during the school year.

Finally, Borman and D'Agostino (1996) noted that across several large-scale evaluations of the federal Title 1 remedial reading program there existed a substantial discrepancy between the reported gains achieved by participating students depending on whether the gains were reported from fall-to-spring or spring-to-spring testing occasions. They wrote,

> The substantially smaller annual gains [spring-to-spring] . . . suggest that the Title 1 intervention during the regular school year alone may not sustain their relatively large Fall/Spring achievement improvements. (p. 323)

In other words, the effects of remedial reading instruction were diminished when the summer vacation period was included in the estimates of achievement growth. Since federal Title 1 funds are targeted to students from low-income families, the summer reading loss phenomenon would produce just such discrepancies in program impact estimates. Recognition of this phenomenon led Borman and D'Agostino to recommend that greater attention be paid to using Title 1 funds to provide alternative summer educational support programs for Title 1–eligible students. However, it seems that few Title 1 programs have actually heeded that advice (Puma, Karweit, Price, Ricciuti, Thompson, & Vaden-Kiernan, 1997).

SOURCES OF THE RICH/POOR ACHIEVEMENT GAP

Poor children have never fared as well as more advantaged children in American schools (Allington, 2010). In recognition of this, Title 1 funding for interventions for economically disadvantaged students was initiated through the Elementary and Secondary Education Act of 1966. The intent was to provide funding for supplementary educational interventions in the hope of narrowing the achievement gap that existed between more- and less-advantaged students (McGill-Franzen & Goatley, 2001). There is evidence that this achievement gap was narrowed between 1966 and 1992 (Grissmer, Kirby, Berends, & Williamson, 1994) by about half (from 50+ points to 27 points). However, the achievement gap has remained unchanged between more and less economically advantaged students since 1992, a period of 20 years. The National Assessment of Educational Progress in reading provides strong evidence of the pervasive nature of this seemingly intractable rich/poor achievement gap. For instance, twice as many (58% versus 27%) poor 4th-grade students, those eligible for free lunches, fell below the Basic proficiency level as students who were not poor, and far fewer poor students (13% versus 40%) achieved the Proficient level as compared with their more advantaged peers (Donahue, Voelkl, Campbell, & Mazzeo, 1999, p. 82). No narrowing of this gap was accomplished by the Reading First initiative (Gamse et al., 2009). Children from low-income families remain just as far behind children from higher-income families in reading proficiency as they were before that program was initiated. Perhaps the manner in which we conceptualize the reasons for this achievement gap is the problem.

There have been a variety of explanations of the rich/poor achievement gap, but many of the most popular explanations seem not to be supported by the various scientific data discussed above. That is, there exists a substantive scientific literature that locates much of the source of the achievement gap outside the school, classroom, curriculum, or instructional program. Nonetheless, there are good reasons to be optimistic about the potential impact of improving the curriculum and instruction in high-poverty schools, if only because so much work has demonstrated the potential that such improvements can make in student achievement (e.g., Hiebert, Colt, Catto, & Gury, 1992; Mathes, Denton, Fletcher, Anthony, Francis, & Schatschneider, 2005; McGill-Franzen, Allington, Yokoi, & Brooks, 1999; Taylor, Pearson, Clark, & Walpole, 2000; Vellutino, Scanlon, Sipay, Small, Pratt, Chen, & Denckla, 1996). It is not that improving the quality of classroom reading instruction can be ignored in attempting to ameliorate the rich/poor reading achievement gap, just that the scientific evidence on the accumulating impact of summer reading loss on the achievement gap is so compelling. What is, perhaps, surprising is just how long that evidence has been largely ignored by educators and policymakers.

The various available data consistently portray summer reading loss as the most potent explanation for the widening reading achievement gap between rich and poor children across the elementary and middle school years. But, as Entwisle et al. (1997) suggested, mandating summer school attendance for children from low-income families may not always be the most appropriate response. At the very least, alternatives to compulsory summer school should be explored, if only for purely economic and ethical reasons. That is, compulsory summer school attendance for students from low-income families would be an expensive response and would also present a potentially discriminatory policy framework.

Volume of Reading Activity and Reading Development

It requires extensive practice to become skilled at almost any activity, whether the activity is more physical or more cognitive in nature (Allington, 2009). In the case of reading proficiency, "literally hundreds of correlational studies find that the best readers read the most and that poor readers read the least. These correlational studies suggest that the more children read, the better their fluency, vocabulary, and comprehension" (National Reading Panel, 2000, p. 12). The absence of experimental studies on the effects of reading volume on reading development is lamented by the National Reading Panel (though Krashen [2001] provides evidence that counters that perceived shortcoming). The ethical and practical difficulties of conducting studies where reading volume is rigorously manipulated over time, especially in the face

of the powerful and consistent correlational and cross-sectional findings, make it unlikely that experimental research on this issue will
soon appear. Nonetheless, the lack of a substantial experimental research base has not restrained the development of theoretical explanations of the summer reading loss phenomenon (Heyns, 2001). However, the available hypotheses tend to be more sociological in nature
and only limited attention has been paid to the role of reading volume
in summer reading development.

The potential role of reading volume in reading development can
be explained, at least in part, by the "self-teaching" hypothesis (Share
& Stanovich, 1995). This theoretical model indicates that adequate de-
coding skills, for instance, are no guarantee of the development of reading proficiency. Developing independent reading proficiencies requires
"opportunities for self-teaching and other factors such as the quality
and quantity of exposure to print . . . " (p. 25). In other words, the self-
teaching model assumes a potentially powerful role for extensive reading, especially extensive, accurate reading (quality of exposure) of texts
since it is through these repeated successful exposures to the letter
patterns common to the English orthography that beginning readers
develop rapid, flexible word identification skills and strategies (Cunningham & Stanovich, 1998).

But extensive reading produces benefits beyond developing students' word recognition skills. As has been well documented, extensive
reading is a powerful vocabulary-building strategy (Nagy, Anderson,
& Herman, 1987; Swanborn & DeGlopper, 1999), a powerful source
for world knowledge and core curricular knowledge (Stanovich, 1993,
2000), and for the development of understandings of complex written
language syntax and story/text grammars (Chomsky, 1972; Krashen,
2004). But better readers seem to reap more of these benefits than poorer readers, perhaps because 1) they read more extensively (National
Reading Panel, 2000), and 2) they more often read texts where they read
with high levels of accuracy (Gambrell, Wilson, & Gantt, 1981; Swanborn & DeGlopper, 1999). Both the quantity, or volume, of reading and
the quality, or accuracy, of that reading, would be important variables
in children's reading development in the self-teaching hypothesis's explanation of the positive impacts of reading volume.

Volume of reading during the summer school vacation period
would seem obviously important to reading development as explained
by the self-teaching model. The summer vacation period corresponds

to roughly one-third of the academic year. The available evidence suggests that were schools to have some children read virtually nothing during the first 3 months of school, for example, the negative effect on reading development would be observable (Allington, 1984; Fisher & Berliner, 1985; Harris & Serwer, 1966; Hiebert, 1983). If some children read virtually nothing during June, July, and August, we might then also expect a negative impact on reading development.

There are correlational data that address the relationship between the volume of summer reading and summer reading loss. According to Heyns (1978, 1987), volume of summer reading was the best indicator of summer reading loss or gain. Children who read during the summer months were less likely to experience summer reading loss and more likely to have their achievement remain steady or to modestly increase. But too many of the poor 6th- and 7th-grade students in her study read little or nothing during the summer months. Too many also experienced a summer reading loss.

Although there are a variety of data that indicate that lower-achieving students, generally, read less outside of school (e.g., Anderson, Wilson, & Fielding, 1988; Donahue et al., 1999; Stanovich, 2000), there seems to be no large-scale study that employed socioeconomic status as a variable in examining out-of-school reading volume. Nonetheless, the research available points toward several factors that suggest why reading during the summer months might be less common among poor children.

First, elementary school children, especially poor children, report getting most of their reading material from the school or classroom library collections (Lamme, 1976) and schools serving large numbers of poor children have smaller, older, and less diverse school and classroom library collections than other schools (Allington, Guice, Michelson, Baker, & Li, 1996; Duke, 2000; McQuillan, 1998; Neuman, 2009). This means that poor children simply have a much more restricted selection of books to read, even during the school year. Children attending high-poverty schools also experience more restricted access to the more limited print resources (Guice, Allington, Johnston, Baker, & Michelson, 1996; McGill-Franzen, Lanford, & Adams, 2002). They not only have fewer books to select from, but they have fewer scheduled visits to the library, more restrictions on how many books can be checked out, and restrictions on whether the books from the school library can be taken home.

Second, beyond the classroom and the school, Neuman and Celano (2001) documented the huge differences in access to children's books in differing communities. Wealthier communities had three businesses selling children's books for every one that existed in poorer communities. But the differences were even worse when they tallied the number of children's book titles available. In the worst-case scenario, they found more than 16,000 books that could be purchased in the wealthier community and 55 books in the poorer one. On every measure of print access, these researchers documented the gaping differences between what was available in richer communities, contrasting those rich print environments with the impoverished situation found in high-poverty neighborhoods. While researchers have often focused on the differences in print access in schools serving rich and poor children, this study powerfully documents the substantial beyond-the-school advantages children living in wealthier communities have.

Third, family income has been shown to be a quite powerful predictor of the number of age-appropriate children's books and magazines that are available in the home (Halle, Kurtz-Costes, & Mahoney, 1997; Neuman, 1986; Smith, Constantino, & Krashen, 1997; Waples, 1937). The lowest-income families have limited fiscal resources and book purchases fall into the discretionary needs category. As Halle et al. (1997) noted:

> Because many of these families cannot afford to purchase children's
> books, it becomes all the more important to make [books] . . . easily and
> readily available within disadvantaged communities. (p. 535)

One might hypothesize that the limited availability of children's books in high-poverty communities is related to the problem of limited discretionary income. Retailers stock what they can sell. If books are discretionary purchases, then differences in retailers' display of books would seem likely related to the amount of discretionary money available to families in different communities. That said, the problem of limited access to books and other reading materials in low-income communities remains—access both in and out of school (McGill-Franzen & Allington, 1993; McGill-Franzen, Allington, Solic, Williams, Zmach, Graff, & Love, 2005; Neuman, 2009).

This access problem is amplified in the summer months, when children typically have no access to the book collections in the schools.

Even in high-poverty schools planning to offer a summer school program, it seems that the school library is too rarely open and available for use and even classroom libraries are often off-limits (unless the classroom teacher is teaching in the summer school program).

Motivation, Reading Activity, and Summer Reading Loss

We should be clear, though, that not every poor child experiences summer reading loss. Poor children exhibit a variety of achievement patterns during the summer months. Puma, Karweit, Price, Ricciuti, Thompson, and Vaden-Kiernan (1997) reported that higher-achieving poor students fared better than lower-achieving students. Lower-achieving poor children demonstrated a greater summer reading loss. While family socioeconomic status and reading achievement is highly correlated, this pattern suggests that poor children's limited access to books during the summer months cannot alone explain the consistent finding of substantial summer reading loss among poor children.

It seems likely that there are any number of motivational and volitional factors (Wigfield, 1997) that influence reading behavior, especially voluntary summer reading activity. For instance, children's efficacy beliefs are linked to past academic performance, including their experiences as more- or less-successful readers. A history of less-successful reading experiences produces a lower sense of self-efficacy in readers than a history of successful reading experiences. The lower sense of self-efficacy then predicts lower levels of engagement in reading, especially voluntary reading (Schunk & Zimmerman, 1997; Wigfield & Guthrie, 1997). And it is the poor reader who is most likely to be assigned texts that are too hard (Allington, 1980; Block, 1980; Gambrell, Wilson, & Gantt, 1981; O'Connor, Bell, Harty, Larkin, Sackor, & Zigmond, 2002), texts they read with little fluency, limited accuracy, and without comprehension. It is poor readers, then, who would seem least likely to exhibit the motivation to read voluntarily—during the school year or the summer months. Greater success in school reading is central to enhancing out-of-school voluntary reading. Thus, there is a need for a dual focus on improving classroom instruction while also addressing the problem of poor children's access to appropriately complex books for voluntary summer reading.

Creating classroom environments where successful reading is the norm—for all children—means creating classrooms where children are well matched to the books they are reading. One-size-fits-all curriculum plans—where every child is to read the same books—cannot produce a consistent pattern of successful reading. Classroom reform efforts will necessarily be targeted to ensuring that all children have books they can read accurately, fluently, and with understanding (McGill-Franzen, 1993). It isn't just the motivational research that offers support for attending to the match (or mismatch) between the text difficulty and student proficiency. There is an extensive research literature linking successful reading experiences (accurate, fluent, high comprehension) to better reading progress (e.g., Allington, 2009; Berliner, 1981; Betts, 1949; O'Connor et al., 2002; Swanson & Hoskyn, 1998). Any intervention focused on stimulating voluntary reading must necessarily be concerned about matching book difficulty to student reading proficiency.

But providing books of appropriate complexity seems to be only the first step in encouraging voluntary reading. There is good evidence that building on student interest can stimulate an interest in reading, even among lower-achieving readers (Guthrie & Anderson, 1999). Central to fostering enhanced interest in voluntary reading is providing a substantial degree of autonomy in the choice of texts to be read and a substantial quantity of books that vary on several dimensions, including difficulty, genre, topic, and length. In an optimal environment, self-selection of books on topics of personal interest, or written by favorite authors, or within a particular genre are all important features of efforts to promote greater voluntary reading, especially among lower-achieving students (Guthrie & Humenick, 2004; Turner, 1995).

From the research available, then, we can conclude:

- There is abundant evidence that summer reading loss is one of the important factors contributing to the reading achievement gap between rich and poor children.
- There is powerful evidence indicating that children from low-income families have more restricted access to books, both in school and out of school, than do their more-advantaged peers.
- There is rich and consistent correlational evidence illustrating that better readers read more than poorer readers, supporting theoretical models that emphasize the importance of the

volume of successful reading experiences in the development of reading proficiency.

- There is a substantial body of research linking successful school reading experiences with the motivation to read voluntarily. Successful school reading experiences require a curriculum framework that emphasizes allowing children to select books to read that are appropriate to their level of reading development.

Given this research, what are the implications for current educational reform initiatives targeted to eliminating the rich/poor reading achievement gap?

RESEARCH-GUIDED REFORM PRINCIPLES

There are at least two broad principles to be drawn from this research that might guide educational reform efforts.

- *First, volume of reading is important in the development of reading proficiency* (Allington, 2009; Krashen, 2006; Pressley, 2006; Stanovich, 2000). Does the reform design ensure that all students read extensively during the school day? (A focus on volume of reading is fundamentally different from a focus on time allocated for reading instruction. Too often, scheduling a 90-minute reading block results in children reading for 10 minutes or less and doing other sorts of work for the remaining 80 minutes.) Does the reform design enhance students' voluntarily reading—in the evenings, on the weekends, and during summer vacations?
- *Second, children must have easy access—literally fingertip access—to books that provide engaging, successful reading experiences throughout the calendar year if we want them to read in volume.* Does the reform design provide classroom book collections so that all students, regardless of their achievement levels, have easy access to hundreds of titles of appropriately difficult books? Does it provide that such an array of books is also available to students every Friday for

take-home weekend reading and also available throughout the summer? Does it provide teachers with the skills needed to match children and books?

Having set forth these two principles, we would note that all children also need consistent access to rich and explicit demonstrations of the thinking that proficient readers do before, during, and after reading. They need access to expert instruction, in other words. We wish it only took blocks of time to read and access to books to foster reading development, but children need to be taught also. But good teaching may go unrewarded if students do not practice those skills and strategies extensively while independently reading appropriately difficult texts (O'Connor et al., 2002). It is during such independent practice that students consolidate those skills and strategies and come to own them. Without regular successful reading practice, reading proficiency seems to suffer a setback.

CONCLUSION

Too many current educational reform initiatives ignore ease of access to books, reading volume, and summer reading loss. This seems especially true for reforms targeted to eliminating the rich/poor reading achievement gap. If all children are to develop thoughtful literacy proficiencies, reform efforts must change. Federal programs, state initiatives, and local reform efforts must be designed to reflect, at the very least, the research-based principles set forth above. Children need an enormous supply of successful reading experiences, both in school and out, to become proficient, independent readers. The potential role of summer voluntary reading in the development of reading proficiency (and in closing the reading achievement gap) has been too long neglected by educators and policymakers. Schools that serve many poor children must play a substantive role in ensuring that each and every child has year-round access to a generous supply of books to read in school and out, books the children cannot wait to read.

REFERENCES

Alexander, K. L., Entwisle, D. R., & Olson, L. S. (2007). Lasting consequences of the summer learning gap. *American Sociological Review, 72*(2), 167–180.

Allington, R. L. (1980). Teacher interruption behaviors during primary grade oral reading. *Journal of Educational Psychology, 72*, 371–377.

Allington, R. L. (1984). Content coverage and contextual reading in reading groups. *Journal of Reading Behavior, 16*, 85–96.

Allington, R. L. (1994). What's special about special programs for children who find learning to read difficult? *Journal of Reading Behavior, 26*, 1–21.

Allington, R. L. (2009). If they don't read much . . . 30 years later. In E. H. Hiebert (Ed.), *Reading more, reading better* (pp. 30–54). New York: Guilford Publishers.

Allington, R. L. (2010). Recent federal education policy in the United States. In D. Wyse, R. Andrews, & J. V. Hoffman (Eds.), *International Handbook of English, Language and Literacy Teaching* (pp. 496–507). New York: Routledge.

Allington, R. L. (2012). *What really matters for struggling readers: Designing research-based programs*, 3rd ed. Boston: PearsonAllynBacon.

Allington, R. L., Guice, S., Michelson, N., Baker, K., & Li, S. (1996). Literature-based curriculum in high-poverty schools. In M. Graves, P. van den Broek, & B. Taylor (Eds.), *The first r: Every child's right to read* (pp. 73–96). New York: Teachers College Press.

Anderson, R. C., Wilson, P., & Fielding, L. (1988). Growth in reading and how children spend their time outside of school. *Reading Research Quarterly, 23*, 285–303.

Berliner, D. C. (1981). Academic learning time and reading achievement. In J. Guthrie (Ed.), *Comprehension and teaching: Research reviews* (pp. 203–225). Newark, DE: International Reading Association.

Betts, E. A. (1949). Adjusting instruction to individual needs. In N. B. Henry (Ed.), *The forty-eighth yearbook of the National Society for the Study of Education: Part II, Reading in the elementary school* (pp. 266–283). Chicago: University of Chicago Press.

Block, J. H. (1980). Success rate. In C. Denham & A. Lieberman (Eds.), *Time to learn*. Washington, DC: National Institute of Education.

Borman, G. D., & D'Agostino, J. V. (1996). Title 1 and student achievement: A meta-analysis of federal results. *Educational Evaluation and Policy Analysis, 18*, 309–326.

Calkins, L., Ehrenworth, M., & Lehman, C. (2012). *Pathways to the Common Core: Accelerating achievement*. Portsmouth, NH: Heinemann.

Chomsky, C. (1972). Stages in language development and reading exposure. *Harvard Educational Review, 42*, 1–33.

Cooper, H., Nye, B., Charlton, K., Lindsay, J., & Greathouse, S. (1996). The effects of summer vacation on achievement test scores: A narrative and meta-analytic review. *Review of Educational Research, 66,* 227–268.

Cunningham, A. E., & Stanovich, K. E. (1998). The impact of print exposure on word recognition. In J. Metsala & L. Ehri (Eds.), *Word recognition in beginning literacy* (pp. 235–262). Mahwah, NJ: Lawrence Erlbaum Associates.

Donahue, P. L., Voelkl, K. E., Campbell, J., & Mazzeo, J. (1999). *NAEP Reading 1998: Reading report card for the nation and the states.* Washington, DC: U.S. Department of Education, Office of Educational Research and Improvement.

Duke, N. K. (2000). For the rich it's richer: Print experiences and environments offered to children in very low- and very-high-socioeconomic status first-grade classrooms. *American Educational Research Journal, 37,* 441–478.

Entwisle, D. R., Alexander, K. L., & Olson, L. S. (1997). *Children, schools, and inequality.* Boulder, CO: Westview Press.

Fisher, C. W., & Berliner, D. C. (1985). *Perspectives on instructional time.* New York: Longmans.

Gambrell, L. B., Wilson, R. M., & Gantt, W. N. (1981). Classroom observations of task-attending behaviors of good and poor readers. *Journal of Educational Research, 74,* 400–404.

Gamse, B. C., Jacob, R. T., Horst, M., Boulay, B., & Unlu, F. (2009). *Reading First Impact Study Final Report (NCEE 2009-4038)* (No. (NCEE 2009-4038)). Washington, DC: National Center for Education Evaluation and Regional Assistance, Institute of Education Sciences, U.S. Department of Education.

Grissmer, D. W., Kirby, S. N., Berends, M., & Williamson, S. (1994). *Student achievement and the changing American family.* Santa Monica, CA: RAND: Institute on Education and Training.

Guice, S., Allington, R. L., Johnston, P., Baker, K., & Michelson, N. (1996). Access?: Books, children, and literature-based curriculum in schools. *The New Advocate, 9,* 197–207.

Guthrie, J. T., & Anderson, E. (1999). Engagement in reading: Processes of motivated, strategic, knowledgeable, social readers. In J. T. Guthrie & D. Alvermann (Eds.), *Engaged reading: Processes, practices, and policy implications* (pp. 17–45). New York: Teachers College.

Guthrie, J. T., & Humenick, N. M. (2004). Motivating students to read: Evidence for classroom practices that increase motivation and achievement. In P. McCardle & V. Chhabra (Eds.), *The voice of evidence in reading research.* (pp. 329–354). Baltimore: Paul Brookes Publishing.

Halle, T., Kurtz-Costes, B., & Mahoney, J. (1997). Family influences on school achievement in low-income, African-American children. *Journal of Educational Psychology, 89,* 527–537.

Harris, A. J., & Serwer, B. L. (1966). The CRAFT project: Instructional time in reading research. *Reading Research Quarterly, 2,* 27–57.

Hayes, D. P., & Grether, J. (1983). The school year and vacations: When do students learn? *Cornell Journal of Social Relations, 17,* 56–71.

Heyns, B. (1978). *Summer learning and the effects of schooling.* New York: Academic Press.

Heyns, B. (1987). Schooling and cognitive development: Is there a season for learning? *Child Development, 58,* 1151–1160.

Heyns, B. (2001). *Summer learning . . . and some are not.* Paper presented at the After the bell: Education solutions outside the school, a conference organized by the New York University Center for Advanced Social Science Research, The Jerome Levy Institute, Bard College, June 4–5.

Hiebert, E. H. (1983). An examination of ability grouping for reading instruction. *Reading Research Quarterly, 18,* 231–255.

Hiebert, E. H., Colt, J. M., Catto, S. L., & Gury, E. C. (1992). Reading and writing of first-grade students in a restructured Chapter 1 program. *American Educational Research Journal, 29,* 545–572.

Krashen, S. (2001, October). More smoke and mirrors: A critique of the National Reading Panel report on fluency. *Phi Delta Kappan,* 119–123.

Krashen, S. (2004). *The power of reading: Insights from the research,* 2nd ed. Portsmouth, NH: Heinemann.

Krashen, S. (2006). Free reading. *School Library Journal, 9,* 42–45.

Lamme, L. (1976). Are reading habits and abilities related? *Reading Teacher, 30,* 21–27.

Lyon, G. R., & Chhabra, V. (2004). The science of reading research. *Educational Leadership, 61*(6), 12–17.

Mathes, P. G., Denton, C. A., Fletcher, J. M., Anthony, J. L., Francis, D. J., & Schatschneider, C. (2005). The effects of theoretically different instruction and student characteristics on the skills of struggling readers. *Reading Research Quarterly,* 40(2), 148–182.

McGill-Franzen, A. M. (1993). "I could read the words!": Selecting good books for inexperienced readers. *Reading Teacher, 46,* 424–426.

McGill-Franzen, A. M., & Allington, R. L. (1993, October 13). What are they to read? Not all kids, Mr. Riley, have easy access to books. *Education Week,* 26.

McGill-Franzen, A. M., Allington, R. L., Yokoi, L., & Brooks, G. (1999). Putting books in the room seems necessary but not sufficient. *Journal of Educational Research, 93,* 67–74.

McGill-Franzen, A., Allington, R. L., Solic, K., Williams, L., Zmach, C., Graff, J., & Love, J. (2005). The rich/poor achievement gap: Contributions of summer reading loss. *Tennessee Reading Teacher, 34*(1), 28–30.

McGill-Franzen, A. M., & Goatley, V. (2001). Title 1 and special education:

Support for children who struggle to learn to read. In S. Neuman & D. Dickinson (Eds.), *Handbook of Early Literacy Research* (pp. 471–483). New York: Guilford.

McGill-Franzen, A. M., Lanford, C., & Adams, E. (2002). Learning to be literate: A comparison of five urban preschools. *Journal of Educational Psychology, 94* (3), 443–464.

McQuillan, J. (1998). *The literacy crisis: False claims, real solutions.* Portsmouth, NH: Heinemann.

Nagy, W., Anderson, R. C., & Herman, P. (1987). Learning word meanings from context during normal reading. *American Educational Research Journal, 24,* 237–270.

National Reading Panel. (2000). *Teaching children to read: An evidence-based assessment of the scientific research literature on reading and its implications for reading instruction.* (http://www.nationalreadingpanel.org).

Neuman, S. (1986). The home environment and fifth-grade students' leisure reading. *Elementary School Journal, 86,* 335–343.

Neuman, S. B. (2009). *Changing the odds for children at risk.* New York: Teachers College Press.

Neuman, S., & Celano, D. (2001). Access to print in low-income and middle-income communities. *Reading Research Quarterly, 36,* 8–26.

O'Connor, R. E., Bell, K. M., Harty, K. R., Larkin, L. K., Sackor, S. M., & Zigmond, N. (2002). Teaching reading to poor readers in the intermediate grades: A comparison of text difficulty. *Journal of Educational Psychology, 94*(3), 474–485.

Pressley, M. (2006). *Reading instruction that works: The case for balanced teaching.* New York: Guilford.

Puma, M. J., Karweit, N., Price, C., Ricciuti, A., Thompson, W., & Vaden-Kiernan, M. (1997). *Prospects: Final report on student outcomes.* Washington, DC: U.S. Department of Education, Office of Planning and Evaluation Services.

Rampy, B. D., Dion, G. S., & Donahue, P. L. (2009). *The nations' report card: trends in academic progress in reading and mathematics, 2008.* Washington, DC: National Center for Educational Statistics, National Assessment of Education Progress, Institute for Education Sciences.

Schunk, D. H., & Zimmerman, B. J. (1997). Developing self-efficacious readers and writers: The role of social and self-regulatory processes. In J. T. Guthrie & A. Wigfield (Eds.), *Reading engagement: Motivating readers through integrated instruction* (pp. 34–50). Newark, DE: International Reading Association.

Share, D. L., & Stanovich, K. E. (1995). Cognitive processes in early reading development: Accommodating individual differences in a model of acquisition. *Issue in Education, 1,* 1–57.

Smith, C., Constantino, R., & Krashen, S. (1997). Differences in print environment: Children in Beverly Hills, Compton and Watts. *Emergency Librarian, 24,* 8–9.

Stanovich, K. E. (1993). Does reading make you smarter? Literacy and the development of verbal intelligence. In H. Reese (Ed.), *Advances in Child Development and Behavior, Vol. 24* (pp. 133–180). New York: Academic Press.

Stanovich, K. E. (2000). *Progress in understanding reading: Scientific foundations and new frontiers.* New York: Guilford.

Swanborn, M. S. L., & DeGlopper, K. (1999). Incidental word learning while reading: A meta-analysis. *Review of Educational Research, 69,* 261–286.

Swanson, H. L., & Hoskyn, M. (1998). Experimental intervention research on students with learning disabilities: A meta-analysis of treatment outcomes. *Review of Educational Research, 68,* 277–321.

Taylor, B. M., Pearson, P. D., Clark, K., & Walpole, S. (2000). Effective schools and accomplished teachers: Lessons about primary grade reading instruction in low income schools. *Elementary School Journal, 101,* 121–165.

Turner, J. C. (1995). The influence of classroom contexts on young children's motivation for literacy. *Reading Research Quarterly, 30,* 410–441.

Vellutino, F. R., Scanlon, D. M., Sipay, E. R., Small, S. G., Pratt, A., Chen, R., & Denckla, M. (1996).Cognitive profiles of difficult-to-remediate and readily remediated poor readers: Early intervention as a vehicle for distinguishing between cognitive and experiential deficits as basic causes of specific reading disability. *Journal of Educational Psychology, 88*(4), 601–638.

Waples, D. (1937). *Research memorandum on social aspects of reading in the depression* (Bulletin # 37). New York: Social Science Research Council. (Reprinted by the Arno Press, New York, NY, 1972)

Wigfield, A. (1997). Children's motivations for reading and reading engagement. In J. T. Guthrie & A. Wigfield (Eds.), *Reading engagement: Motivating readers through integrated instruction* (pp. 14–33). Newark, DE: International Reading Association.

Wigfield, A., & Guthrie, J. T. (1997). Relations of children's motivations for reading to the amount and breadth of their reading. *Journal of Educational Psychology, 89,* 420–432.

CHAPTER 2

Interventions That Increase Children's Access to Print Material and Improve Their Reading Proficiencies

James J. Lindsay

OTHER CHAPTERS IN this book present a research-based argument for giving books and other types of print material to children growing up in low-income families. The argument includes four research-based premises:

- There exist poverty gaps in reading achievement, as evidenced by state and national data (National Center for Education Statistics, 2009).

- Data collected on preschoolers and from preschoolers' parents suggest that poverty-related achievement gap in reading begins prior to children's entry into the school system (e.g., O'Donnell, 2008).

- For school-aged children, data from numerous studies suggest that income-related achievement gaps in reading get larger due to loss of reading skills among children living in poverty during the summer months (Cooper, Nye, Charlton, Lindsay, & Greathouse, 1996).

- Children living in poverty have less access to books and other print material in their homes, in their classrooms, in their school libraries, and in their community libraries than children not living in poverty (e.g., Allington, Guice, Baker, Michelson, & Li, 1995; Neuman & Celano, 2001).

The conclusion is based on these premises: Providing books and other types of print material to children living in poverty may facilitate either shared reading between caregivers and children or increased reading among children themselves (i.e., increase the volume of reading). Such increased reading may help improve these children's reading achievement. For school-aged children—so the argument goes—access to books is especially important during the summer months, during which time they are unable to obtain books from their classroom or school libraries.

Although this logical argument may appear compelling, nothing is as compelling as *direct evidence* that programs that facilitate children's access to print material actually improve their performance on various education-related outcomes. Our research team at Learning Point Associates (which has since merged with American Institute for Research) was contracted by Reading Is Fundamental (RIF) to conduct an exhaustive and systematic review of the research on children's access to print material and children's outcomes in order to address the following four research questions:

1. When examining all research studies conducted on the relationship between access to print material and various children's outcomes, what is the overall effect size for these relationships?

2. Do the studies designed to examine causal relationships between access to print material and children's outcomes show positive effects?

3. Do studies examining programs that facilitate children's ownership of print material in particular (as opposed to programs supporting the lending of reading materials to children) show impacts on various behavioral, educational, and psychological outcomes?

4. Finally, do certain characteristics of studies (e.g., research designs used, types of samples of children, types of contexts, types of programs, types of outcomes) relate to the strength of the relationships between access to print materials and children's outcomes?

In other words: How big a difference does access to books make in reducing summer reading loss, does it matter whether those materials are owned or borrowed by children, and do some kinds of studies of access to reading materials show a stronger impact than others on children's reading? In this chapter, I present a summary of the methods used for this research review as well as the overall findings that emerge when findings from relevant studies are combined through meta-analysis.

APPROACH USED IN THE META-ANALYTIC REVIEW

The review that our research team conducted on behalf of RIF was unlike others performed previously on this subject (e.g., McQuillan, 1998; McQuillan & Au, 2001) in its comprehensiveness, its systematic and transparent screening and coding process, its focus on rigorous studies for discerning impact, and its use of meta-analytic techniques to arrive at overall impact estimates across studies. In short, the project team designed this research review to be as scientifically sound as possible so as to withstand the scrutiny of other educational researchers and policymakers. A general summary of the methods used in this research review is provided here.[1]

Searching for All Possible Studies on Children's Access to Print and Outcomes

Research reviews can be cursory or comprehensive, depending on the lengths to which reviewers go to obtain potentially relevant research reports. On the one hand, reviewers can enter a few keywords into their favorite research literature database (e.g., EBSCO, ERIC) and maybe find a few studies that address the topic. Reviewers taking this approach may be overlooking research reports that are not listed in that particular database, and may therefore be making conclusions based on just some of the relevant studies. Our review team took another approach. We consulted with a research librarian to create a list of *all* possible research literature databases that may include descriptions of reports related to the subject of children's access to print material and outcomes. We also worked with the librarian to develop a comprehensive string of search terms that would identify any study that was potentially relevant. In the end, our team searched 16 different research databases for reports related to the topic. This search found 11,503 potentially relevant research reports.

While searches of *all* relevant research literature databases may yield many potentially relevant studies, it is still possible that reviewers may miss studies that address the subject. Literature databases only include reports of studies that have been published in books, journals, government reports, and compendia of conference presentations. However, the literature databases may not contain reports of unpublished studies that often contain "null findings" or findings that are not statistically significant (Lipsey & Wilson, 2001; Rothstein, Sutton, & Borenstein, 2005). Thus, reviews that fail to attempt to locate unpublished studies (i.e., those in researchers' file drawers or computer hard drives) may indicate effects that are larger than are really the case. Our review team attempted to locate such unpublished studies by sending inquiries about such "hard-to-find studies" to researchers who may have done work on this topic (directly and through a broadcast email sent to members of the Literacy Research Association). This approach yielded seven additional research reports.

Finally, for each research report that was screened by our review team, we checked the studies referenced in the report against our master list of studies obtained through database searches and contacts with

researchers. References not in our master list were added. This additional approach yielded 106 more reports.

In sum, we identified 11,616 research reports that were potentially
relevant to the subject. These reports were then screened to ensure
that they were relevant to the subject of the review and that they con-
tained findings from primary research (i.e., did not duplicate findings
in other reports).

Screening Research Reports for Relevance and Primary Research Findings

A screening process was created for these research reports to ensure
that information regarding specific findings was ignored when deciding
whether to include or exclude particular reports. After removing the 96
"duplicates" (studies cited in multiple databases or obtained through
multiple approaches), the reports were screened to make sure they addressed the subject of children's access to print material and one or more
outcomes and to make sure that they provide the findings of primary
research (i.e., were empirical research reports). A team of screeners first
examined the one-paragraph summary abstracts of the research reports
and made judgments about whether the report was relevant and empirical. Only reports that screeners agreed were relevant and "empirical"
were included, and those for which there was uncertainty or inconsis-
tency in judgments continued to the next round of screening. That next
round—screening of full text versions of reports—was conducted in a
similar manner. The project manager was the final arbiter for reports for
which there were disagreements among screeners. The project manager
also screened out any reports of studies that did not employ research designs that allowed even rudimentary calculations of relationships (e.g.,
pre–post studies without comparison group, satisfaction surveys). The
final number of empirical and relevant research studies that emerged
from this systematic screening process was 108.

Coding Studies and Calculating Effect Sizes

In addition to determining the overall impact of interventions that
increase children's access to print material, this project was designed to
look at study factors that may moderate the magnitude of impacts (i.e.,
settings and populations for whom the interventions are most effective;

components that increase effectiveness of the interventions). To do so, key features of the 108 research reports were coded. The team coded report-related information (e.g., type of publication outlet, authors, whether published or unpublished), characteristics of the research design used, characteristics of the intervention that provided children with access to print (if applicable), characteristics of the sample (e.g., number of boys and girls, grade level/age of children, racial/ethnic status of children, socioeconomic status of the children, primary language of children), and characteristics of the research setting (e.g., whether study was conducted in the United States). Research design information allowed the review team to distinguish studies that were *rigorous* (studies that allow researchers to conclude that an intervention *caused* changes in outcomes) from non-rigorous studies (studies that only indicate relationships between children's access to print and outcomes, without supporting a direction of causality).

Research findings for each independent sample of children were then translated into a single metric or effect size: the mean standardized difference.[2] These mean standardized differences can be negative (suggesting that access to print corresponds with poorer performance on an outcome), positive (indicating that access to print corresponds to improved performance), or close to zero (suggesting no relationship between access to print and outcomes). By examining the magnitude of effect sizes (rather than looking exclusively at statistical significance of findings), educators and policymakers can determine the anticipated "bang" produced by an intervention per the "bucks" that go into implementation.

Synthesis of Findings and Categorization of Outcomes

All meta-analytic procedures used for this review were consistent with the latest research and scholarly opinion among meta-analytic experts (e.g., Cooper, Hedges, & Valentine, 2009). These procedures include "reining in" extreme effect sizes, weighting effect sizes by the number of children in the independent sample, and adjusting weights to accommodate nested data and random effects. Generally speaking, these adjustments make findings *more conservative* (i.e., closer to zero). Once proper weights are calculated, average weighted effect sizes are calculated for each outcome to determine the overall effect for a given outcome category. Confidence intervals indicate the probable range of "true" effects. If confidence intervals include the value of zero, one cannot be confident that a relationship exists.

During the coding process, reviewers cataloged 58 different types of outcomes that have been linked within the reviewed studies to children's access to print material. To simplify analysis and reporting, we grouped these outcomes into eight categories:

1. *attitudes* toward reading (e.g., children's liking or disliking of books and/or reading),
2. *motivation* to read (e.g., children's interest in reading, requesting to be read to or to go to a library),
3. *reading behavior* (e.g., amount of time children spend reading, frequency of reading, book-related play, home literacy orientation),
4. *basic language skills* (e.g., children's ability to understand language and to express language),
5. *emergent literacy skills* (e.g., children's ability to identify letters, to produce the sounds related to letters, to track print from left to right, to identify words),
6. *reading performance* (e.g., reading fluency, comprehension, vocabulary, teachers' judgments of students' reading levels),
7. *writing performance* (e.g., length of writing sample, structure of the sample, grammar, spelling, vocabulary used), and
8. *general academic performance* (i.e., a catchall category for other indicators of performance, including grades/GPA, achievement in subjects other than reading, grade promotion/retention, achievement gaps).

Research questions are answered by reporting meta-analytic findings for the various categories of outcomes.

META-ANALYTIC FINDINGS

There are no universally agreed-upon standards for categorizing the magnitudes of effect sizes, although effect sizes are typically the way that the results of a meta-analysis are reported. What we can do is compare the average effect sizes found in this review with benchmarks derived from effects from other interventions. One set of benchmarks for examining magnitude of effects is the "rules of thumb" that were first devised by Jacob Cohen, the methodologist who introduced the notion of standardized mean difference or *d-index* (Cohen, 1988). Based on his knowledge of research in the social sciences, Cohen classified effect sizes smaller than .20 as "small," effect sizes between .20 and .80 as "medium," and effects greater than .80 as "large."[3] These rules of thumb may help readers interpret the findings presented.

The research review findings are presented according to the overarching research questions mentioned previously. Another way to view the presentation of findings is in terms of the set of research reports that were collected during the search process, the subset of studies that met the criteria for rigor (i.e., high-quality studies of interventions that either *lend* books/print material to children or *give* books/reading material to children), and the mostly overlapping subset of studies that focus exclusively on interventions that give books to children (commonly referred to as book distribution programs or book giveaway programs). The relationships between these subsets of studies are presented graphically in Figure 2.1. Following presentation of findings for these three sets of research studies, I will briefly present possible moderating factors that may affect the magnitude of impacts (focusing on just rigorous studies).

Relationships Between Children's Access to Print Material and Outcomes

The first set of analyses focused on the overall relationships between children's access to print material and the eight different outcome categories (i.e., the overall pool of studies illustrated in Figure 2.1). The analyses included findings from large correlational studies about children's reading activities (e.g., Hall & Coles, 1999), findings from data collected as part of the National Assessment of Educational Progress/the Nation's Report Card (e.g., Foertsch, 1992), findings from large international studies (e.g., Progress in International Reading and Literacy Study—PIRLS; Myrberg & Rosén, 2008), and findings from the more rigorous studies of specific interventions that facilitate children's access to print materials.

Findings from the meta-analyses show positive relationships between children's access to print material and each of the eight categories of outcomes (see Table 2.1). In short, children who have greater access to print material are more likely to have better attitudes toward

FIGURE 2.1. Groupings of Research Reports Corresponding to Research Questions

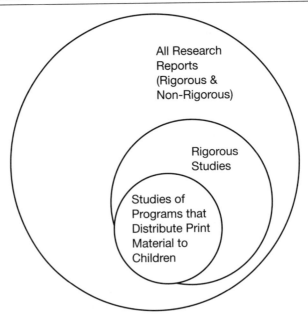

reading, are more motivated to read, tend to read more, have better language development, show stronger emergent literacy skills, show stronger reading and writing skills, and demonstrate better overall academic achievement. In other words, easy access to books is a critical aspect in producing proficient readers.

While the meta-analytic findings in Table 2.1 suggest that *interventions* that increase children's access to print material *may* help improve the various education-related outcomes, readers must remember that these average effect sizes only reflect general relationships taken across all studies—rigorous and non-rigorous. It may be that for some of the outcomes, the direction of causality may run in the opposite direction (e.g., children who are more motivated to read may purposely surround themselves with print material). Alternatively, these relationships may exist due to their connections with an unmeasured third variable, such as family income. To get a clearer picture regarding whether *interventions* that facilitate children's access to print actually *cause* these outcomes, separate meta-analyses must be run on the subset of studies that used rigorous research designs (i.e., designs that allow causal inferences).

TABLE 2.1. Relationships Between Children's Access to Print Material and Outcomes

Outcome Category	Number of Independent Samples	Average Weighted Effect Size
Attitudes toward reading	27	+0.333*
Motivation to read	15	+0.617*
Reading behavior	41	+0.704*
Basic language abilities	34	+0.400*
Emergent literacy skills	50	+0.330*
Reading performance	106	+0.441*
Writing performance	17	+0.393*
General achievement	40	+0.543*

* signifies that confidence intervals do not include value of 0.

Causal Connections Between Lending and Giveaway Programs and Outcomes

The definition of "rigorous" that our review team used when characterizing the research designs used in studies closely corresponded with standards adopted by the U.S. Department of Education's *What Works Clearinghouse* (U.S. Department of Education Institute of Education Science, 2008).[4] To be considered "rigorous" for our review, studies must have included random assignment of children, classrooms, or schools to intervention conditions (i.e., some receive greater access to books and some do not) or researchers must have attempted to equate intervention conditions prior to the study in an unbiased way (i.e., employed a strong quasi-experimental design). Studies that simply compared groups of students, classrooms, or schools without attempting to show equivalence of these "units" on other potential causal factors were not considered rigorous. The research community agrees that inferences of causation can only be based on these types of rigorous studies (Shadish, Cook, & Campbell, 2002).

Another round of meta-analyses was done using findings from just these rigorous studies (see the smaller subset in Figure 2.1). Findings are presented in Table 2.2. As can be seen, the meta-analytic findings show that interventions that lend print materials (e.g., books and magazines) to children or give print materials to children *cause* improved

TABLE 2.2. Findings from Rigorous Studies on Children's Access to Print Material and Outcomes

Outcome Category	Number of Independent Samples	Average Weighted Effect Size
Attitudes toward reading	12	+0.336*
Motivation to read	3	+0.16
Reading behavior	11	+0.589*
Basic language abilities	15	+0.128
Emergent literacy skills	19	+0.499*
Reading performance	29	+0.267*
Writing performance	10	+0.099
General achievement	1	n/a

* signifies that confidence intervals do not include value of 0.

attitudes toward reading, increased reading behavior, improved emergent literacy skills, and improved reading performance. The average effect sizes for motivation to read, language development, and writing performance were also positive, yet the meta-analytic findings suggest that we cannot be 95% confident that the causal relationship is positive. Note that the finding on children's motivation to read is based only on three research studies. Only one rigorous study was found that examined non-reading-related outcomes (McCormick & Mason, 1986), and so no meta-analytic findings are provided for the category of general achievement.

Impacts of Book Distribution Programs and Children's Educational Outcomes

The findings just presented indicate that interventions that facilitate children's access to print material (book lending programs and giveaway programs) *cause* improvements in psychological outcomes (attitudes), behavioral outcomes (reading behavior), and educational achievement outcomes (emergent literacy skills and reading performance). The next set of findings focus on those types of programs and interventions that are most like Reading Is Fundamental: programs that give books and other types of print materials to children for free.[5] As indicated in Figure 2.1, nearly all studies that comprised this sub-

TABLE 2.3. Findings from Studies of Book/Print Distribution Programs and Outcomes

Outcome Category	Number of Independent Samples	Average Weighted Effect Size
Attitudes toward reading	4	+0.384*
Motivation to read	2	+0.967*
Reading behavior	14	+0.568*
Basic language abilities	15	+0.140
Emergent literacy skills	16	+0.442*
Reading performance	12	+0.435*
Writing performance	7	+0.257
General achievement	1	n/a

* signifies that confidence intervals do not include value of 0.

set would be classified as rigorous. Findings do not change when non-rigorous studies are removed from this analysis.

Meta-analytic findings for this subset of studies were in most ways similar to those for the larger subset of rigorous studies (lending and giveaway programs, combined). Giving books and other types of print material to children (e.g., high-interest magazines) *causes* more favorable attitudes toward reading, greater "volume" of reading, better emergent literacy skill development, and better reading performance (see Table 2.3). Unlike the previous analysis, giveaway programs also appear to improve children's motivation to read.[6]

Factors That May Increase or Decrease Intervention Impacts

The meta-analytic review also examined whether particular features of studies, samples, or interventions were related to the magnitude of effects. This type of moderator analysis can provide researchers, program developers, and those charged with implementing these types of interventions with *hints* regarding the circumstances, settings, populations, or intervention features associated with larger impacts. However, readers are cautioned against placing too much stock in these moderator findings, since moderating features tend to overlap within studies (i.e., are "confounded"; Lipsey, 2003) to such an extent that one cannot always tell which moderating feature within a study is contributing to effects. Additional research will help clarify which features are most influential on impacts.

The moderator findings presented in Table 2.4 suggest that moderators in the rigorous studies do not influence the outcome categories in a uniform way.[7] Those charged with setting up book lending or giveaway programs can either focus on the type of outcome that they are most interested in improving (i.e., the columns in Table 2.4) or determine the predominant finding for each moderator (i.e., the rows).

Notable among these moderator findings is the indication that programs that provide encouragement and guidance to caregivers have larger impacts. That is, book lending or giveaway programs that also encourage caregivers to co-read with their child, provide guidance on *how* to read with their child (e.g., dialogic reading techniques; Whitehurst, Arnold, Epstein, Angell, Smith, & Fischel, 1994) or provide information on "scaffolding" reading support with their child (Kim & White, 2008) have larger impacts than do book lending/giveaway programs that lack these directions. Impacts are also larger when the distribution of books/print material is combined with other literacy activities (e.g., McGill-Franzen, Allington, Yokoi, & Brooks, 1999).

Magnitude of Impacts

The findings thus far: Programs that facilitate children's access to print material produce positive impacts on children's psychological, behavioral, and educational outcomes (see Table 2.1). This statement is based on statistical significance of meta-analyzed findings. However, policymakers and school and community leaders may be more interested in whether these impacts are large enough to justify the expense. I attempt to address this question next by providing benchmarks against which to view the magnitude of the meta-analytic findings.

Given the earlier classification of effect sizes, four of the average impacts found for rigorous studies in our review lie in the "medium" range, and three would be considered small. The effect for the most policy-relevant outcome category—reading performance—falls in the medium range.

Increasing Access to Books Produces Larger Achievement Gains Than Many Other Interventions

Another set of benchmarks for comparing meta-analytic findings is the average impacts among educational interventions conducted in elementary schools, middle schools, and high schools. Lipsey's (2010)

TABLE 2.4. Summary of Moderator Analysis Findings (Rigorous Studies)

Moderator Type/Moderator	Attitudes	Motivation	Reading Behavior	Basic Language Skills	Emergent Literacy Skills	Reading Performance	Writing Performance	General Academic Achievement
Sample and Setting								
% male	—	—	—	—	—	—	—	—
% in poverty	—	—	—	—	—	—	—	—
% minority	—	negative	negative	—	positive	negative	—	—
% nonnative speakers	—	—	—	—	—	—	negative	—
School level	—	best at younger ages	best at younger ages	best in elementary grades	best in Pre-K & K	best in K, positive in all but Pre-K	no interpretation	—
Intervention								
Choice of materials	—	choice < no choice	choice < no choice	—	choice > no choice	—	choice > no choice	—
Children's eligibility	—	all children < "eligible children"	all children > "eligible children"	—	—	—	—	—
Number of materials	—	best with more materials	—	—	—	—	best with fewer materials	—
Distribution intervals	—	best with shorter intervals	best with longer intervals	—	—	best with shorter intervals	best with longer intervals	—
Caregiver guidance	—	guidance > no guidance	guidance > no guidance	guidance < no guidance	guidance > no guidance	guidance > no guidance	guidance < no guidance	—
Encouragement to read	—	encouraged > unencouraged	encouraged > unencouraged	encouraged < unencouraged	encouraged > unencouraged	encouraged > unencouraged	—	—
Sponsor	—	multiple and clinic > schools	multiple and clinic > schools	preschool > others	no interpretation	—	other > school	—
Combined with other literacy activities	—	other activities > no activities	other activities > no activities	—	other activities > no activities	—	—	—

analysis shows that on average, interventions have had impacts of .14, .11, and .10 standard deviations in elementary schools, middle schools, and high schools, respectively (see Figure 2.2). Comparison of these impacts with the impacts from the rigorous studies examined in our meta-analysis shows that in general, interventions that facilitate children's access to print material produce impacts that are one to four times as large as those in the average intervention (depending on the outcome category being examined). The more policy-relevant outcome—reading performance—showed impacts that are about twice as large as the average impact found in elementary schools.

At the very least, these benchmark comparisons indicate that book lending and book distribution programs work and that the magnitude of impacts is not trivial. The responsibility for deciding whether the "bang" (impact) created by book lending and distribution programs is sufficient to justify the "bucks" (resources) lies with policymakers and community leaders.

SUMMARY AND IMPLICATIONS
FOR PREVENTING SUMMER READING LOSS

In this chapter, I have described an extensive meta-analytic review of the research on children's access to print materials and outcomes. The review incorporated a systematic and multipronged approach to uncover every research study ever conducted on the subject. The process for screening research reports prevented reviewers' biases from influencing decisions of whether studies should be included. Moreover, the meta-analysis procedures used are those that are currently recommended by experts in the field. Some of those procedures result in more conservative findings. In short, everything was done to ensure that the meta-analytic findings represent the totality of research findings on the subject and that our biases and the biases of our sponsor could not enter into the meta-analytic results.

The results confirm the intuitive belief held by many educators: Providing books and magazines to children—either by lending the materials to them or by giving them the materials to keep—improves their attitudes toward reading, the amount of reading that they do, their acquisition of basic literacy skills, and their reading performance. Impacts for children's motivation to read, basic language skills, and

FIGURE 2.3. Comparison of Findings with Those from Other Educational Interventions

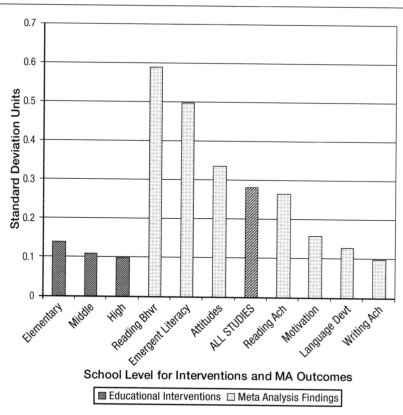

writing achievement all point in the positive direction as well; however, we cannot say with certainty that interventions that increase children's access to print material improve that subset of outcomes. Although the evidence suggests positive impacts for just giving books/ print material to children, impacts are even larger when provision of reading material accompanies supplemental literacy instruction and directions to caregivers.

These findings suggest that book lending and giveaway programs may aid in closing the gaps in achievement between children growing up in upper-/middle-class families and those who grow up in lower-class families. Such gaps begin before children enter school (O'Donnell, 2008) and widen throughout the school years. Part of the widening of income-related achievement gaps can be attributed to the loss of literacy skills that children in lower-income families demonstrate during the summer months (Chapter 1, this volume; Cooper, Nye, Charlton, Lindsay, & Greathouse, 1996). Findings from our meta-analytic review suggest that book lending and distribution programs enacted during the summer months and targeted to children living in lower-income families may prevent the widening of gaps in reading achievement (Allington, McGill-Franzen, Camilli, Williams, Graff, Zeig, Zmach, & Nowak, 2010).

NOTES

1. Many of the details are omitted because they are inappropriate in a chapter like this. However, readers wanting more information are free to examine the full technical report, which is available from the author. Correspondence regarding this chapter can be sent to Jim Lindsay, American Institutes for Research, 1120 East Diehl Road, Ste 200, Naperville, IL, 60563 or through email: jlindsay@air.net.

2. The mean standardized difference (sometimes called a d-index) represents the difference between average score for the intervention group and the average score of a comparison group, divided by the pooled standard deviation of the two groups.

3. This general classification was supported by Lipsey's evaluation of 186 meta-analyses of educational, psychological, and behavioral interventions (Lipsey, 1990).

4. *What Works Clearinghouse* classifies studies that randomize units to conditions as *meeting evidence standards*, and studies that attempt to create equivalent groups as *meeting evidence standards, with reservations.*

5. The interventions that were tested within this subset of studies had this "print material giveaway" feature in common with RIF's largest program, their "books for ownership" program. However, RIF's program has other components as well: targeting of schools that serve high-need children, emphasis on children's choice of age-appropriate, prescreened books, and encouragement of sites to pair book distribution days with family/community events focused on reading. Our search for research studies found no studies that directly tested the efficacy of RIF's *Books for Ownership* program.

6. Despite the "statistically significant" finding for motivation (confidence intervals do not include zero), we remain cautious in making conclusions for this outcome category. Our caution is based on two factors: 1) we are not completely satisfied with the way in which motivation is defined in the studies we reviewed, and 2) this particular meta-analytic finding is based only

on two studies. Clearly, more work needs to be done to examine whether book giveaway and lending programs foster children's motivation to read.

7. These moderator findings focus on *rigorous* studies only.

REFERENCES

Allington, R., Guice, S., Baker, K., Michelson, N., & Li, S. (1995). Access to books: Variations in schools and classrooms. *The Language and Literacy Spectrum, 5,* 23–25.

Allington, R. L., McGill-Franzen, A., Camilli, G., Williams, L., Graff, J., Zeig, J., Zmach, C., & Nowak, R. (2010). Addressing summer reading setback among economically disadvantaged elementary students. *Reading Psychology, 31*(5), 411–427.

Cohen, J. (1988). *Statistical power for the behavioral sciences* (2nd ed.). Hillsdale, NJ: Erlbaum.

Cooper, H., Hedges, L. V., & Valentine, J. C. (Eds.). (2009). *The handbook of research synthesis and meta-analysis* (2nd ed.). New York: Sage.

Cooper, H., Nye, B., Charlton, K., Lindsay, J., & Greathouse, S. (1996). The effects of summer vacation on achievement test scores: A narrative and meta-analytic review. *Review of Educational Research, 66*(3), 227–268.

Foertsch, M. (1992). *Reading in and out of school.* Washington, DC: National Center for Education Statistics, U.S. Department of Education.

Hall, C., & Coles, M. (1999). *Children's reading choices.* New York: Routledge.

Kim, J. S., & White, T. G. (2008). Scaffolding voluntary summer reading for children in grades 3 to 5: An experimental study. *Scientific Studies of Reading, 12*(1), 1–23.

Lipsey, M. W. (1990). *Design sensitivity: Statistical power for experimental research.* Newbury Park, CA: Sage.

Lipsey, M. W. (2003). Those confounded moderators in meta-analysis: Good, bad, and ugly. *Annals of the American Academy of Political and Social Science, 587*(1), 69–81.

Lipsey, M. W. (2010). *Beyond p-values: Characterizing education intervention effects in meaningful ways.* Paper presented at the IES Research Conference, National Harbor, MD.

Lipsey, M. W., & Wilson, D. B. (2001). *Practical meta-analysis.* Thousand Oaks, CA: Sage.

McCormick, C., & Mason, J. M. (1986). *Use of little books at home: A minimal intervention strategy that fosters early reading* (Technical Report No. 388). Champaign, IL: Center for the Study of Reading. Retrieved June 26, 2010, from http://www.eric.ed.gov/PDFS/ED314742.pdf

McGill-Franzen, A., Allington, R. L., Yokoi, L., & Brooks, G. (1999). Putting books in the classroom seems necessary but not sufficient. *Journal of Educational Research, 93*(2), 67–74.

McQuillan, J. (1998). *The literacy crisis: False claims, real solutions.* Portsmouth, NH: Heinemann.

McQuillan, J., & Au, J. (2001). The effect of print access on reading frequency. *Reading Psychology, 22,* 225–248.

Myrberg, E., & Rosén, M. (2008). A path model with mediating factors of parents' education on students' reading achievement in seven countries *Educational Research and Evaluation, 14*(6), 507–520.

National Center for Education Statistics. (2009). *The Nation's Report Card: Reading 2009* (NCES 2010–458). Washington, DC: Institute of Education Sciences, U.S. Department of Education.

Neuman, S., & Celano, D. (2001). Access to print in low-income and middle-income communities. *Reading Research Quarterly, 36*(1), 8–26.

O'Donnell, K. (2008). *Parents' reports of the school readiness of young children from the National Household Education Surveys Program of 2007* (NCES 2008-051). Washington, DC: National Center for Education Statistics, Institute of Education Sciences, U.S. Department of Education. Retrieved from http://nces.ed.gov/pubs2008/2008051.pdf

Rothstein, H. R., Sutton, A. J., & Borenstein, M. (2005). *Publication bias in meta-analysis: Prevention, assessment and adjustments.* Chichester, UK: Wiley.

Shadish, W. R., Cook, T. D., & Campbell, D. T. (2002). *Experimental and quasi-experimental designs for generalized causal inference.* Boston: Houghton-Mifflin.

U.S. Department of Education Institute of Education Science. (2008). *What works clearinghouse: Procedures and standards handbook (version 2.0).* Washington, DC: Author. Retrieved November 11, 2010, from http://ies.ed.gov/ncee/wwc/references/idocviewer/doc.aspx?docid=19&tocid=1

Whitehurst, G. J., Arnold, D. S., Epstein, J. N., Angell, A., L., Smith, M., & Fischel, J. (1994). A picture book reading intervention in day care and home for children from low-income families. *Developmental Psychology, 30,* 679–689.

CHAPTER 3

What Have We Learned About Addressing Summer Reading Loss?

Anne McGill-Franzen
Richard L. Allington

GIVEN WHAT WE know about the contributions of summer reading loss to the rich/poor reading achievement gap, this chapter describes a number of research projects that have addressed summer reading loss and the outcomes of these studies. These outcomes are heartening because in each and every study, simply increasing poor children's summer access to books that matched their reading development levels has produced reading growth and the elimination of summer reading loss. If there is a problem with this research, it is simply that too few such studies exist. Nonetheless, we believe these studies establish a much-needed framework for considering how to close the rich/poor reading achievement gap.

SUMMER VOLUNTARY READING STUDIES

In a series of studies Anne McGill-Franzen and Dick Allington and their colleagues (Allington & Guice,1996, 2003; McGill-Franzen & Allington, 2003, 2008; McGill-Franzen & Love-Zeig, 2008; Allington, McGill-Franzen, Camilli, Williams, Graff, Zeig, Zmach, & Nowak, 2010) and James Kim and his colleagues (2004, 2006, 2008; White & Kim, 2008, 2010) have demonstrated the potential of voluntary summer reading programs in addressing summer reading loss. The stimulating research that pushed this agenda was cited in the opening chapter, but we must give a special nod to Barbara Heyns (1978, 1987), whose work 30+ years ago demonstrated the importance of summer reading activity in reducing or eliminating summer reading loss. Heyns demonstrated correlationally that poor children did not read much during the summer but that when they did read voluntarily during the summer months, reading loss largely disappeared. However, as clear as her correlational studies were, we could find no evidence that anyone had experimentally attempted to address summer reading setback.

Although correlational studies are important, correlations alone do not identify cause and effect relationships. Heyns had provided the correlational evidence showing that poor kids who read voluntarily during the summer were far less likely to experience summer reading loss. The question that is begged, however, is whether better readers simply read more than struggling readers. That is, with correlational data there is always the problem of establishing the direction of the correlation. However, planning a study of voluntary reading or planning studies that attempt to increase the amount of voluntary reading that children do are fraught with problems.

First, there is the issue of fairness. Is it fair to provide some children—in this case, some poor children—with a supply of books for voluntary reading while also having a control group who are not provided such books? In our view, it was unfair but providing books to some students is both a moral issue and a financial issue. For instance, if we had the funding we would provide all children, rich and poor, with all the books they needed for voluntary reading. But we are not billionaires;

instead, we were able to obtain funding to provide some books to some poor children in our experimental study. We used federal grant funding to purchase a supply of books for some of the poor children enrolled in 17 high-poverty schools in Florida. In order to examine the effects of providing these books for summer reading on reading achievement, we also randomly identified some of the poor children in the same schools to serve as our control group. That is, we did not provide these children in the control group with books to read over the summer.

The good news concerning our study, and those done by Kim and his colleagues as well, is that providing poor children with self-selected books for summer reading did improve the reading achievement of the children receiving the books when we compared it with the reading achievement of the poor children to whom we did not provide books. In fact, the amount of reading growth we observed in the children we gave free books to proved at least as large as the growth others have found in sending poor children to summer school (Cooper, Nye, Charlton, Lindsay, & Greathouse, 1996; Cooper, Charleton, Valentine, & Muhlenbruck, 2000). Consider that distributing a dozen self-selected books to poor children produced positive effects on reading achievement that equaled the effects provided by attending summer school! Our cost was less than $50 per student each year. Summer school costs a lot more. But our effort produced just as much growth in reading achievement.

So What Did We Do?

We created a spring book fair, providing about 500 titles each year for the book fair. We ran the book fairs for 3 consecutive years. The students were in grades 1 or 2 when we began and in grades 3, 4, or 5 when the study ended (some students were in grade 3 due to retention in grade). These students attended schools where between 68 and 98% of all students qualified for free or reduced-price meals. Most students were African American (89%) and a few were Caucasian (5%). The remaining students were Hispanic but from a variety of Caribbean or Latin American countries. Although we selected more students initially, we concluded our study with 852 students receiving free summer books for each of the 3 years, and 478 students remained in the control (no books) group. In both groups, we lost approximately 25% of the students we began with. We lost these students because they moved out of the schools where we conducted the study (though some of these students moved to one of the other schools participating in the study). There were no significant differences in the two groups in terms of ethnicity, reading level, or free-lunch status when we began the study (although the free-books group had more children eligible for free lunch, it was not statistically significant).

The Books We Provided

We selected books for our study in four broad categories:

- *Popular series*—Here, we selected several titles from the most popular series books (as indicated by sales figures). Examples included *Junie B. Jones, Captain Underpants, Goosebumps,* and *Animorphs.*
- *Popular culture*—These books featured characters and topics that were current in the broader popular media (television, movies, athletes, musicians, and so on). Examples in this category included books about Spider-Man, Scooby-Doo, Poké-mon, Hilary Duff, and the Rock.
- *Culturally relevant*—This category included books by minority authors and/or featured minority characters. Examples included *The Gold Cadillac; Little Bill; Sojourner Truth; Forty Acres and Maybe a Mule,* and *Aunt Flossie's Hat* and *Crab Cakes Later.*
- *Curriculum relevant*—Each year, we reviewed the state science and social studies standards for topics that would be studied by the participants the following school year. We then selected titles that fit those topics. Examples included *Medieval Times; Mummies, Tombs, and Treasures; From Tadpoles to Frogs; Into the Rain Forest.*

Most frequently selected books:

1. *Hangin' with Destiny's Child*
2. *Hangin' with Lil' Romeo: Backstage Pass*
3. *Pop People: Lil' Romeo*
4. *Hangin' with Hilary Duff*
5. *The Captain Underpants Extra Crunchy Book of Fun*

5. *The Adventures of Super Diaper Baby*

7. *Harry Potter and the Goblet of Fire*

8. *What Did I Do to Deserve a Sister Like You?*

8. *The All New Captain Underpants Extra Crunchy Book of Fun*

8. *Meet the Stars of Professional Wrestling* (from Williams, 2008).

Our students selected books more often from the first two than from the last two categories. In fact, the ten most popular titles each year were from either the popular series or popular culture book options. We were surprised, but after much discussion we concluded that there is something we would call "kid culture" that led to these choices. In other words, in the world of children there are influences that all children are affected by and these include both television and movies and popular culture factors such as fast-food restaurants and grocery store merchandise. In all of these aspects children, all children, are exposed to certain trends, people, and themes. During the period we did our study, for instance, movies such as *Ice Age* and *Scooby-Doo* came out and were featured in products from fast-food restaurants. In addition, Hilary Duff was the star of a popular television series and the Rock became a movie star after leaving his professional wrestling career. In addition, the series books are simply among the most popular books children read if we judge primarily from book sales figures.

Book Fairs

Each April, we scheduled book fairs in each of the 17 high-poverty elementary schools. We brought the books in clear plastic bins organized according to topic, genre, and series. Once we had set up the book displays, usually in a school library or cafeteria, we invited the children selected to receive free summer books down to visit the book fair. We invited approximately 15 children at a time. Once the children arrived, we introduced the book ordering form, which had spaces for entering 15 different three-digit numbers that identified the books they wished to receive for summer voluntary reading. We then quickly introduced the various book bins and had the children begin exploring their options.

Each year, we varied the titles available, although we repeated some of the most popular titles. We selected books based primarily upon the reading levels of the children each year. These high-poverty schools produced many children reading below grade level, so the selection of books each year always considered that fact. In addition, we were interested in selecting books that these kids could read independently. If many of the 2nd-grade students were still reading at a 1st-grade level, we had to provide a sufficient supply of books in each category that could be read independently. We mention this because too often we hear educators emphasizing reading books at the instructional level. Although books of such difficulty are appropriate for small, guided reading groups where the children participate before, during, and after reading scaffolding and lessons, instructional level books are, in our view, simply too hard for children to read independently.

Book Difficulty

Our project then targeted books that these children could read at their independent level (99% accuracy with phrasing and expression). However, we allowed children to select their own books with only modest advice from us or our colleagues. Our advice was almost always requested ("Do you have any vampire books?"). We randomly selected roughly 100 students to review their book choices with them and to have them read a brief portion of five texts aloud to us. This meant we could see whether most children selected mostly books that they could read independently.

What we found is that the most struggling readers were the children who most often selected books they could not read accurately. Sometimes, this was because they selected the book without actually sampling the text. That is, they saw the cover and it looked interesting, so they selected the book. Or they saw a high-achieving student select a book (let's say a book from the *Harry Potter* series) and they then also selected it. What we learned here was that selecting books for themselves to read was not something struggling readers were very adept at doing. Perhaps this is because they rarely select the texts they will read. Whatever the reason, more struggling readers selected too-hard books. Some children asked to replace these books after we had them try to read a bit of them. We allowed the children this option if they requested it.

However, what we generally found was that most of these children did a good job of selecting books they could read accurately and fluently. And our analyses showed that when children selected books

Independent-, Instructional-, and Frustration-Level Books

Too often, poor readers struggle with their reading because their school reading experiences do not follow the research evidence. Thus, too many struggling readers are placed in grade-level readers (or given grade-level tradebooks) that represent texts at their frustration level. This violates everything we know about effective reading instruction. For their reading lessons, all students need to have texts at their instructional levels. All kids also need much successful, independent practice with reading if we expect them to become proficient readers. All readers then need much independent level reading activity. This independent reading should occur every day both in school and in their homes. Teachers and schools can and must, in our view, work hard at ensuring that adequate independent reading activity occurs at school and at home, and, we argue, over the summer vacation months.

For determining whether children are reading books at the appropriate level, use the accuracy and fluency levels below.

Independent level: Reads with 99% accuracy and in phrases with expression and 90% comprehension.

Instructional level: Reads with 95 to 98% accuracy mostly in phrases with 75% comprehension.

Frustration level: Reads with less than 95% accuracy and often word by word with comprehension below 75%.

Drawn from: Allington, R. L. (2012). *What really matters in response to intervention*. New York: Allyn, Bacon.

well matched to their reading levels, they made greater reading gains than when they selected books that were too difficult or too easy. The question is how to best ensure that children only select the books they can read accurately and fluently. Had we organized the book fairs such that children with similar reading proficiencies attended the book fairs together, we might have been better able to control the difficulty level of the books the children selected. But that would have created more intrusions into the school day. We might have asked the children to be sure to open each book they were considering and try reading a couple of pages just to see if it too easy or too hard. But we had assumed that children had already acquired such skills through their visits to the school libraries. Obviously, at least for some children, we were wrong.

However, some students selected books for others as well as for themselves. When we asked children why they selected certain books, we were initially surprised when a child told us, "My little sister really likes Clifford books; that's why I picked these two." We hadn't planned on providing books for other members of a child's family. Nonetheless, children's responses led us to believe that in many cases, books were selected for other family members (or, in some cases, for friends, who were unfortunately assigned to the control group that was not supposed to be receiving summer books).

Why Choice Is Important in Summer Books Projects

Unlike most other summer books projects, we allowed children free rein to select whichever books they wanted to read. We did this because of the powerful research evidence on the role of self-selection, or free choice. Consider that in a large-scale meta-analysis of access to books, Lindsay (2010) found that the effect size on reading achievement for access when choice was involved was $d = .766$, but substantially smaller ($d = .402$) when students did not choose the texts they were given. Thus, providing access to summer books with choice produced effects on reading achievement almost twice as large versus access without choice (someone else selected the books to be distributed). This only makes sense to us because outside of school few of us ever read books someone else assigns us to read. Providing students with the opportunity to select the books they will read begins the preparation of literate adults, adults who know how to find books they want to read.

Reading Logs

We also provided participating students with a book log to record their summer reading activity and a prepaid and addressed envelope for returning the log to us. This reading log was simply a collection of pages where children were asked to draw something from the book and write a sentence about their drawing. They were also asked to answer two questions, one about how difficult the book was (too easy, about right, too hard) and about interestingness (boring, okay, very good).

Unfortunately, most students never returned their reading logs. In retrospect, we needed a different scheme to attempt to monitor

Summary Book Log

Circle your answer to both questions.

This book was:

   easy to read

   about right

   too hard to read

This book was:

   very good

   okay

   boring

Below draw a picture of a favorite part of the book. Write a sentence that tells what the picture shows.

summer reading. We are reasonably sure, as parents of five children, that some of these reading logs never made it home. Others made it home, but were never noticed by the child's parent or caregivers. Or they were brought home, noted by a parent or caregiver, but over the period of summer vacation the logs were lost or misplaced and thus never returned.

We wish we had had a better return rate for the reading logs. This is because the students who returned the logs exhibited substantially larger gains than did the whole sample. That is, the effect size of the summer books on reading development was twice as large for those students who returned their reading logs. But when fewer than 20% of the children return their logs, we are left with less reliable data than we wanted. It is possible that the children who returned their logs were children from homes where parents or caregivers were more involved with their children over the summer months. If that is so, then returning the logs tells us something else. When parents are more involved, summer voluntary reading is more powerful. Nonetheless, those children who returned their reading logs are the only children that we can be sure actually read the books they selected. Our findings, reported below, are for all children who received summer books, not just for the children whom we know had read those books.

Our Findings

We used student performances on the state reading achievement test given the year our project ended. We found statistically significant differences in reading achievement between the groups and a statistically significant effect size indicating that providing self-selected summer reading materials improves reading achievement (Allington et al., 2010; McGill-Franzen & Allington, 2008). The overall effect size on reading achievement was d = .14, the same size impact as was reported for attending summer school (Cooper et al., 2000).

These results suggest one approach to addressing the rich/poor reading gap. It is a cost-effective approach at roughly $50 per child per year. Given that many schools already spend much more than this on unproven schemes (test preparation, computer-based interventions, commercial reading programs) in an attempt to improve reading scores, it would seem that this effort is replicable in every district that educates poor children.

FINDINGS FROM OTHER SUMMER READING STUDIES

In another effort, Anne McGill-Franzen and Jackie Love-Zeig (2008) developed a summer reading/writing strand for use in traditional summer schools. They report on two summer school projects organized around the Summer Reading Club model. In each summer school, teachers allocated from half an hour to 1 hour to the Summer Reading Club activities during their summer school classes. In both summer schools, Summer Reading Club participants gained more in reading levels and text reading accuracy and fluency than the control students who attended summer school in the same schools but in programs that did not include Summer Reading Club for the same amount of time (half-days for 4 or 5 weeks).

Teachers were provided with text sets on bugs and sea life in the Summer Reading Club classes. How kids K–3 used illustrations (cutaway drawings, timelines, lists) to support their learning from multiple texts was the general focus of these studies. They point to drawing as one way to motivate struggling readers during summer school activities.

Kim has also demonstrated the positive effects of summer voluntary reading on reading achievement. His initial nonexperimental study (Kim, 2004) reported a multivariate regression analysis on a school-sponsored voluntary summer reading program targeted to 6th-grade students in 18 high-poverty elementary schools. In this effort, the school district provided students with a list of more than 100 books that students could read during the summer months. Students were to write a book report on the books read. However, only a minority of students completed the book reports (45% of Caucasian students, 28% of Black students, and 22% of Hispanic students actually completed the assignments).

The distribution of light, moderate, and heavy readers was almost equal across ethnic groups. In this study, it was found that reading four or five books over the summer was sufficient to stem summer reading loss with these 6th-graders. The .12 effect size for reading four or five books indicates that summer reading of a sufficient number of books raised reading achievement at a level commensurate with attending summer school. But this study also presents the problem of attaining student participation in a district-mandated program of voluntary reading. Here, only 16% to 36% of parents, responding differentially by ethnic groups, signed the verification notice. For every ethnic group, the majority of parents ignored the district verification notice.

Kim (2006) then conducted an experimental study on the effects of summer voluntary reading. In this case, almost 500 4th-grade students from 10 elementary schools were involved (252 treatment and 234 control students). The treatment students received eight books weekly, delivered by mail over the summer months. All students in both groups participated in a set of lessons at the end of the academic year preceding the summer reading. These lessons focused on five comprehension strategies over 2 weeks and an introduction to a paired reading activity where they selected short passages from their texts to read aloud to a peer. These lessons were delivered by their classroom teachers at the end of the school year in order to prepare students for independent summer reading. Kim created a computer-based algorithm that included reading preferences and reading level of each student. This algorithm selected books for children. He found a marginally significant effect for providing books for summer reading overall. He found that Black and Hispanic students gained more from participation than did White or Asian students. The largest effects were found for students who scored below the median on the ITBS (Iowa Test of Basic Skills) pretest and the children who reported owning the fewest books. There were no reported positive effects for White students, students owning more than 50 children's books, or for children with above-average scores on the ITBS. Kim (2006) concludes, "This study provides experimental evidence that confirms the robust relationship between reading achievement and voluntary reading of books outside of school" (p. 348).

Kim and White (2008) followed the original study with a more complex study design. In this case, they used 400 students in grades 3, 4, and 5 who were randomly assigned to one of four experimental conditions: control, books only, books with oral reading scaffolding, and books with oral reading and comprehension scaffolding. The books children received were selected to match the child's expressed interests and reading levels. Children in this study were pretested and posttested on the ITBS. Results showed that children in the books with oral reading and comprehension scaffolding condition scored significantly higher on the ITBS post-test than children in the control condition. In addition, children in the two scaffolding conditions combined scored higher on the ITBS post-test than children in the control and books only conditions combined.

This study indicates that teachers can prepare students for summer voluntary reading in ways that extend that reading's effects on achievement. Just a few days of instruction supplying students with guidance on both oral reading and comprehension made summer voluntary reading even more effective.

White and Kim (2008) provide several recommendations for summer voluntary reading. These include:

Before the summer begins:

- Teach several lessons that model use of comprehension strategies and oral reading practice with a parent or family member.

During the summer:

- Provide at least eight books closely matched to each student's reading level and interests.
- Send a postcard with each book to remind students that they should read the book and complete the reading log and return it.

Summer reading gains demonstrated
in multiple summer free books studies

Typical summer books program eliminated 3 months of reading achievement loss typical in children from low-income families.

Typical summer reading growth observed in these studies was 3 months' reading gain.

Total impact of free summer books programs was 6 months' reading gain when compared with reading achievement of control group (no books) children.

- Send a letter to parents asking them to listen and provide feedback on a student's reading, by asking children to tell them about the book, the characters, the problem, and their thoughts about the book. Ask that the postcards be returned so you can see the program is being implemented as intended. (p. 124)

They also note that all students in these studies made an average growth of 2.5 months in reading achievement over the summer months they were involved in this summer voluntary reading program, and low-income students grew 4 months.

Shin and Krashen (2008) report on a summer books project embedded in a summer school program for struggling 6th-grade readers. Both the experimental and control group children attended summer school for 4 hours daily over a 6-week period. The control group teachers largely used the same curriculum materials as they did during the school year, and focused primarily on skills development although they did provide 20 minutes of self-selected reading time each day. The experimental group had 25 minutes of library time, 80 minutes of self-selected reading, 45 minutes of literature-based instruction using a whole-class tradebook approach, 45 minutes of project activity (linked to reading and writing), and 25 minutes of teacher read-aloud from children's books.

Because control kids scored higher on the pretest of reading achievement compared with the experimental kids, an ANCOVA (Analysis of Covariance) was used to examine the effects of the summer reading program. On the post-test, the experimental students significantly out-performed the control students (13 months' versus 2 months' gain). This study found, then, that summer school programs that dramatically increased the time children spent engaged in reading self-selected books along with peer discussions of what they were reading produced large gains when compared with the gains shown when children participate in traditional summer school activities.

SUMMARY

Thus, we have several studies of voluntary summer reading programs, all showing positive effects on student reading proficiency. Single-year studies report smaller levels of growth than the one longer-term study. Studies where teachers are provided professional development on summer reading instruction produce better results than studies where teachers have less involved plans. Plans that involve parents produce greater gains than those that do not.

Perhaps what is most fascinating about these studies is their consistency. Just increasing the amount of voluntary reading that children, especially poor children, do during the summer months adds reading growth. This is even more important when we consider the evidence that children from low-income families typically lose reading proficiency over the summer months. Another way to consider these findings is to note that these efforts eliminated summer reading loss and added several months of summer reading growth. By eliminating summer reading loss and by producing small reading achievement gains, these studies improved poor children's reading achievement by about 6 months every summer!

The evidence available indicates that children from low-income families typically lose 2 or 3 months of reading proficiency every summer (Cooper et al., 1996, 2000). Other evidence suggests that the same summer setback occurs for struggling readers regardless of their family socioeconomic status. But these summer voluntary reading studies indicate that such loss can be stemmed, and stemmed with only a modest investment by school districts, basically by providing free books of appropriate difficulty and linked to student interests for summer reading, or by modifying existing summer school programs to substantially expand the volume of self-selected reading children do during their summer school experience.

If we are serious about eliminating the reading achievement gap between more and less economically advantaged students, then we must seriously consider the findings reported in this chapter. All school districts could provide much assistance to encourage self-selected summer voluntary reading. But few school districts currently provide any of the options researchers have explored.

REFERENCES

Allington, R. L., & Guice, S. (1996). Something to read: Putting books in their desks, backpacks, and bedrooms. In P. H. Dreyer (Ed.), *Visions and realities in literacy (Yearbook of the 60th Claremont Reading Conference)* (pp. 1–16). Claremont, CA: Claremont Graduate School.

Allington, R. L., & McGill-Franzen, A. M. (2003). The impact of summer loss on the reading achievement gap. *Phi Delta Kappan, 85*(1), 68–75.

Allington, R. L., McGill-Franzen, A. M., Camilli, G., Williams, L., Graff, J., Zeig, J., Zmach, C., & Nowak, R. (2010). Addressing summer reading setback among economically disadvantaged elementary students. *Reading Psychology,* 31(5), 411–427.

Cooper, H., Charleton, K., Valentine, J. C., & Muhlenbruck, L. (2000). *Making the most of summer school: A meta-analytic and narrative review* (Vol. 65, No.1). Ann Arbor, MI: Society for Research in Child Development.

Cooper, H., Nye, B., Charlton, K., Lindsay, J., & Greathouse, S. (1996). The effects of summer vacation on achievement test scores: A narrative and meta-analytic review. *Review of Educational Research, 66*(3, Fall), 227–268.

Heyns, B. (1978). *Summer learning and the effects of schooling.* New York: Academic Press.

Heyns, B. (1987). Schooling and cognitive development: Is there a season for learning? *Child Development, 58*(5), 1151–1160.

Kim, J. (2004). Summer reading and the ethnic achievement gap. *Journal of Education of Students at Risk, 9*(2), 169–189.

Kim, J. S. (2006). Effects of a voluntary summer reading intervention on reading achievement: Results from a randomized field trial. *Educational Evaluation and Policy Analysis, 28*(4), 335–355.

Kim, J. S., & White, T. G. (2008). Scaffolding voluntary summer reading for children in grades 3 to 5: An experimental study. *Scientific Studies of Reading, 12*(1), 1–23.

Lindsay, J. (2010). *Children's access to print material and education-related outcomes: Findings from a meta-analytic review.* Naperville, IL: Learning Point Associates.

McGill-Franzen, A., & Allington, R. (2001). Lost summers: For some children, few books and few opportunities to read. *Classroom Leadership On-Line, 4*(9). Retrieved from www.ascd.org

McGill-Franzen, A. M., & Allington, R. L. (2003). Bridging the summer reading gap. *Instructor, 112*(8), 17–18 & 58.

McGill-Franzen, A., & Allington, R. L. (2008). Got books? *Educational Leadership, 65*(7), 20–23.

McGill-Franzen, A., & Love-Zeig, J. (2008). Drawing to learn: Visual support for developing reading, writing, and concepts for children at risk. In J. Flood, S. B. Heath, & D. Lapp (Eds.), *Handbook of research on teaching literacy through the communicative and visual arts* (Vol. II, pp. 399–411). New York: Lawrence Erlbaum Associates.

Shin, F. H., & Krashen, S. D. (2008). *Summer reading: Program and evidence.* New York: PearsonAllynBacon.

White, T. G., & Kim, J. S. (2008). Teacher and parent scaffolding of voluntary summer reading. *Reading Teacher, 62*(2), 116–125.

White, T. G., & Kim, J. S. (2010). Can silent reading in the summer reduce socioeconomic differences in reading achievement? In E. H. Hiebert & D. R. Reutzel (Eds.), *Revisiting silent reading: New directions for teachers and researchers.* (pp. 67-91). Newark, DE: International Reading Association.

Williams, L. M. (2008). Book selections of economically disadvantaged Black elementary students. *Journal of Educational Research, 102*(1), 51–63.

CHAPTER 4

The Importance of Book Selections

Enticing Struggling Readers to Say, "I Want to Read That One!"

Lunetta Williams

WHY DO BOOK SELECTIONS MATTER?

AT ONE OF the Title 1 schools in the Summer Book Project conducted by Allington and McGill-Franzen and their team and discussed in Chapter 3, Sean, a verbose 3rd-grader dressed in clothes that barely fit him, shared his appreciation of being able to choose books that he found motivating.

> *Lunetta:* So tell me, what'd you think about the book fair?
>
> *Sean:* I think it was great, and I like when we get to pick our own books to read. 'Cause some books other people

> pick we [3rd-grade students] don't like, 'cause we like start
> readin' it, and it be like, sometimes it be startin' off stupid.

After hearing Sean's response, I predicted that many students would agree. I know that I agree with Sean. I need to choose my own books if I am going to read voluntarily. When someone else picks books for me, I rarely like them, especially if the person hardly knows me.

The power of choice cannot be underestimated in book selections. Unsurprisingly, researchers found increased task engagement when students were allowed to make learning choices (Deci & Ryan, 1985; Turner, 1995). If children make choices about their reading materials, they feel empowered (Hunter, 2001) and may participate in voluntary reading. On the other hand, if they do not make choices about what they read, they may feel like the book selected for them is a "done deal" and merely get through the book, or pretend to get through the book, with little to no interest.

At least initially, some students may need support from their classroom teacher to find books they want to read. One characteristic of effective teachers is the ability to work with students so that they do find such books. Again, initially, some students seem to benefit from having what we call "reduced choices." This is when their teacher selects three to five books that they can read and books the teacher thinks will be of interest to the reader. Selecting the book you want to read from three to five options is simply an easier task than selecting a book from all the books that are available. In any event, remember that selecting the "right" book is a skill that children develop, with teacher support, over a period of time. Remember, too, that acquiring the ability to self-select a book that is both of interest and of the appropriate level of difficulty is a critical early literacy proficiency.

Considering that many students choose books for voluntary reading from the school or classroom library (Fleener, Morrison, Linek, & Rasinski, 1997; Krashen, 2004; Lamme, 1976), it is imperative that educators discover what books students find interesting so that there is access to these materials at school. One way to discover students' interests is noting books that students self-select. Another way is to listen to students talk about why they selected books during informal talks with peers or during formal individual interviews about book selections.

The National Center for Education Statistics (2010) found that successful readers simply read more. Students, particularly struggling readers, would most likely read for longer and more frequent periods of time if they played an active role in book choice (Worthy, Moorman, & Turner, 1999).

CONTEXT OF THIS BOOK SELECTION STUDY

During the final year of the Summer Book Project, I gained insight into the book selections of an often neglected population in book selection studies, economically disadvantaged Black students (Williams, 2008), who are often labeled as struggling readers (National Center for Education Statistics, 2010). Participants included approximately 300 Black students who attended 1 of 10 urban schools in Florida, with 75% to 96% of the students qualifying for free or reduced-price meals. Participants were between the ages of 8 and 12, and there was almost equal representation of girls and boys.

Students selected 15 books, 12 of which they would own at the end of the project, and 3 of which served as substitutes for out-of-stock books, during book fairs located at their schools. Small groups of approximately 15 students engaged in a shopping-type atmosphere that allowed them to freely converse with their peers and browse through hundreds of books at their leisure as they self-selected books that they would receive, free of charge, during the last week of school.

TOP 10 MOST OFTEN SELECTED BOOKS

After approximately 300 students self-selected 15 books, the following books were among the top 10 most frequently chosen:

10. *How to Draw Spider-Man* (Scholastic Inc., 2003a)
9. *Captain Underpants and the Big, Bad Battle of the Bionic Booger Boy, Part 2: Revenge of the Ridiculous Robo-boogers* (Pilkey, 2003a)
8. *The Captain Underpants Extra-Crunchy Book O' Fun* (Pilkey, 2001)
7. *The All New Captain Underpants Extra-Crunchy Book O' Fun #2* (Pilkey, 2002)
6. *What Did I Do to Deserve a Sister Like You?* (Medearis, 2002)

5. *The Adventures of Super Diaper Baby* (Pilkey, Beard, & Hutchins, 2002)

4. *Hangin' with Hilary Duff* (Scholastic Inc., 2003b)

3. *Pop People: Destiny's Child* (Glass, 2001)

2. *Pop People: Li'l Romeo* (Morreale, 2003)

1. *Hangin' with Li'l Romeo* (Walsh, 2002)

According to this list, participants most often self-selected books that reflected media and mass marketing interests. Half of the books' main characters such as Lil' Romeo, Destiny's Child, Hilary Duff (otherwise known as Lizzy McGuire, the star of a past show on the Disney Channel), and Spider-Man are widely known due to their exposure through movies, television, the radio, and video games, media sources that heavily impact kids' lives. All but one of the top 10 most often selected titles, *What Did I Do to Deserve a Sister Like You?* (Medearis, 2002), can be labeled as mass media because they are all series books. The most popular series of the book fairs by far was Dav Pilkey's *Captain Underpants*. The main characters of this series written in comic book form are two boys, Harold and George, who create their own comic books. Captain Underpants, otherwise known as Mr. Krupp, the principal of their school, is the protagonist of their comic books. At the snap of his fingers, Mr. Krupp takes off all of his clothing except for his underpants and flies away to combat evil. Books in the series usually include flip-o-ramas and sections that instruct readers in drawing some of the characters, and many Summer Book Project participants treasured these features.

The top 10 list indicates that we cannot overlook "kids' culture," which often reflects kids' multimedia worlds such as television shows, movies, and music (Allington, 2012). By far, these books were the ones that students got the most excited about as they shopped for books. Eyes lit up. Voices raised in excitement as one student would say to another (across the room), "Hey, guess what? They have Lil' Romeo." It was apparent that tapping into "kids' culture" was key to get kids interested in reading voluntarily.

The top four most frequently preferred books were nonfiction, which is an atypical finding of a book selection study. Fiction books have commonly been more favored among book selection studies' participants. Simpson (1996) noted that participants in book selection studies may prefer fiction books because most teachers are female and are inclined to emphasize fictional reading. Doiron (2003) and Simpson (1996) agreed that classroom and school libraries often contain more fiction than nonfiction books, and students may prefer fiction books over nonfiction books because of their familiarity with them. The top four books were biographies of people reflected in "kids' culture," and perhaps if the books were fiction and included these same people as characters, they would have been selected just as much. Nonetheless, it was exciting to witness that biographies of celebrities prevalent in "kids' culture" could entice participants to read voluntarily.

HOW STUDENTS TALKED ABOUT SELECTED BOOKS

When reading many book selection studies, it seems as though researchers often use *what* students selected to read and infer *why* they chose certain books (Williams, 2004). This tactic allows researchers, not students, to answer a critical question: Why do students choose particular books? In this study, students provided data about why they selected books through think-alouds and individual interview responses.

Think-Alouds

During the time that each group of students shopped for books to self-select, several participants were individually tape-recorded by the use of wireless microphones, transmitters, and receivers that sent audio signals to separate cassette decks. Before the students chose books, I informed each of the 40 participants (part of the approximate 300 students who provided the top 10 data) to think aloud about their book selections as they shopped. I informed students to "just be yourself and talk about what you are thinking as you look at and choose books today." Also, I modeled how I would think aloud if I were selecting several books that were not included in the book fair.

A more comfortable way of thinking aloud for many participants was talking with their peers who were also selecting books at the book fair. Therefore, not only were students' individual think-alouds recorded, but informal peer discussions were also captured on tape. I transcribed students' talk and coded reasons that they discussed when selecting books.

Individual Interviews

After students selected books, I individually interviewed 30 of the 40 participants who completed think-alouds. During this time, each student responded to open-ended questions such as, "Tell me about why you chose these books that you get to keep." The goal was for students to talk as much as they could, as candidly as they could, about each of the selected books. I transcribed participants' responses and coded the reasons that they offered about selecting books.

WHAT DID STUDENTS SAY ABOUT SELECTED BOOKS?

As to be expected, students had a lot to say about why they selected their books. As I report three of the most commonly stated reasons in this section of the chapter, I suggest that we continue to remember that all students are individuals. There were a few students who did not report some or all of these reasons when describing their book selections. In other words, results of book selection studies such as this one provide guidance, and not a quick fix, for us to use in helping our students become better readers.

Media and Mass Marketing Influences: Give Me Books About Musicians and Superheroes

Musicians featured in the four most often selected books were a topic that participants often mentioned, particularly with their peers, as they all shared similar background knowledge about these famous people. As Miranda selected *Hangin' with Hilary Duff* (Scholastic Inc., 2003b), she discussed her admiration of this star with peers.

Miranda: Okay . . . ah! Oh! She [Hilary Duff] is so cute! Look at um her momma and daddy.

Peer 1: Where?

Peer 2: Look at her friend.

Miranda: Na ah . . . her friend right there.

Peer 1: Her friend. Oh, I saw that show.

Miranda: I know.

Peer 1: I saw the movie.

Miranda: I saw this movie.

Overall, participants seemed infatuated with the musicians' appearances and musical talents and wanted to learn more about them. Often, students would flock to a book about a musician and chorally read excerpts about the intricacies of the person's daily life. It was as if book clubs were forming right under our eyes during the book fairs; students were commonly interested in a particular musician and wanted to read to learn more about him/her. Furthermore, it appeared to be "cool" to be reading and learning more about this topic.

Superheroes were the other characters represented in coveted books during the Summer Book Project, largely due to the influence of media and mass marketing. Male participants were more verbal than females about why they selected books about superheroes. Similar to participants' admiration of musicians' talents, boys were noticeably impressed with the superheroes' strength and supernatural powers and with the power that these abilities provide them to help others and defend themselves. For example, in the below excerpt, Marcus explains why he likes the Incredible Hulk.

Marcus: I like the Incredible Hulk 'cause he helps save the day. And when, like, when somebody try to hurt him, he defends himself.

Captain Underpants was another superhero of many participants' interest. Although this character has not been featured through a media source, the *Captain Underpants* book series has been successful through mass marketing. As McGill-Franzen (1993) noted, students enjoyed the familiarity of the format, characters, and setting of the *Captain Underpants* series. They also particularly enjoyed the bathroom humor and activities within the book such as the flip-o-ramas and word puzzles. Below, Jason talks about a variety of book features that he planned to enjoy when reading a selected *Captain Underpants* book.

Jason: Here go a word search puzzle. This is how you draw Captain Underpants and this [is] the maze. This [is] the comic book and here go the word search puzzle and here go how to draw the turbo toilet.

Other People: What You Read and Do Impacts My Book Selections

Frequently, other people such as adults at school, family, and friends were a source of students' familiarity with selected books. Others had provided access to certain books, read books in front of participants, talked about books to participants, or reminded participants of a book's topic or fictional character. Shila informed me that her teacher served as a source of familiarity for one of her selected books, *A Bad Case of Stripes* (Shannon, 1998), by reading it aloud to the class.

> *Lunetta: A Bad Case of Stripes.* Why did you choose that?
>
> *Shila:* 'Cause it was a favorite book to me.
>
> *Lunetta:* How did you learn about that book?
>
> *Shila:* When my teacher read it to us. 'Cause it shows you how you get stripes and get other kind of colors like checkers, a checkerboard, like that, and the American flag.

In the below excerpt, Deionica explained that she thought she would like *Captain Underpants and the Big, Bad Battle of the Bionic Booger Boy, Part 1: The Night of the Nasty Nostril Nuggets* (Pilkey, 2003b) because her sister enjoyed reading the *Captain Underpants* series.

> *Deionica:* Captain Underpants, um, my sister, she kind of read him and we have one at home, and I just wanted to read—see more about Captain Underpants.

Joshua's father came to mind as he selected *The History Channel Presents the Real Scorpion King* (Banks, 2003). In fact, similar to several Summer Book Project participants, he decided to give the book to his father as a gift.

> *Lunetta:* So what about *The Real Scorpion King?* Tell me about why you got that book.

Joshua: I got that for my daddy 'cause he like watchin' the movies and *Scorpion King* and all that. We had the movie.

Comparable to the notion that book clubs were forming about books reflective of media and mass marketing interests during the book fairs, students appeared to be connecting with others (teachers, family, and friends) outside of the book fairs with books they were selecting to own. Their connections with others and shared interests influenced their book selections and may have also been reflective of a high value placed by their family or community culture on sharing good fortune, in this case, free books.

Life Experiences: I Want to Read About Where I've Been and Where I Want to Go

Sometimes, students selected books because they were reminded of personal experiences. Purves and Beach (1972) stated, "People tend to get more involved in that which is related to them, and they tend to seek the work with which they can identify, or the character who resembles them" (p. 18). Questions that students may wonder about when selecting books include: "How did the character handle a situation similar to mine?" "What did he end up doing after living with a family like mine?" These are questions that students may wonder about when selecting books. Chris, a student in the Summer Book Project, explained his connection to a character in a book she selected.

Lunetta: Tell me about why you chose *What Did I Do to Deserve a Sister Like You?*
Chris: Because she's kind of like me and stuff because I always boss my little sister around.

Several students chose books because they connected with plans for the future, or "where they wanted to go" when they grew up. For example, Jarvis chose several books that related to possible careers. From being a Super Bowl hero to becoming the first Black president, Jarvis had dreams about his future, and he hoped some of his selected books would give him more insight. Below, Jarvis's transcripts reveal his dreams and their relationship to a book that he chose.

Lunetta: So You Want to Be President. Tell me about that.

Jarvis: I want to become maybe the first Black president if I get like higher than football.

Lunetta: I think you totally should go for it. I'll vote for you if I'm still alive, okay?

Jarvis: I'll pray for you.

Lunetta: You'll what?

Jarvis: Pray for you.

I was shocked by Jarvis's responses. As a 4th-grader, he was already thinking about what he would do after high school graduation (something I did not do as a 7th-grader, much less a 4th-grader), and he had hopes for a career outside of sports. Hopefully, the books from the Summer Book Project in addition to all of the other books that Jarvis will be exposed to at school will help him achieve his dreams, even "higher than football."

IMPLICATIONS

Based on the data collected from participants' talk about the top 10 most selected books, during think-alouds and during individual interviews, the following five suggestions could be used to increase the likelihood that children will voluntarily read: 1) gain insight into "kids' culture;" 2) provide access to books reflective of "kids' culture;" 3) allow time for students to build reading communities; 4) broaden students' familiarity with books, and 5) include books that speak to students' lives and futures.

1. Gain Insight into "Kids' Culture"

The findings from this study revealed that books reflective of "kids' culture," particularly media and mass marketing interests, may provide motivation for students to read voluntarily. Educators should continually be aware of "kids' culture" so that they can make reading materials reflective of those interests accessible in classroom and school libraries. The following list provides ideas in gaining insight about "kids' culture."

- Notice what books students self-select in a school or classroom library; note what they bring to school to read from home or the public library.

- Listen to students converse with one another about "kids' culture." Look at what students are wearing (e.g., publicity t-shirts) or items that they bring to school such as spiral notebooks or binders with celebrity or superhero pictures on them.

- Johns and Lenski (2005) provide several examples of interest surveys that can gather insight into "kids' culture," and they do not take long to administer and analyze.

- Simply initiate conversations with students individually. Informally, ask them what they like to do for fun, what interests them, and what they would like to read about when walking to lunch or after school.

2. Provide Access to Books Reflective of "Kids' Culture"

After obtaining information about "kids' culture," provide access to books that reflect this culture and will make students say, "Ooooo. I want that book!" (This was a common expression of participants in this study when they saw the four most commonly selected books.) Although not advocating the *replacement* of classics and award-winning books with books reflective of "kids' culture," this study would suggest the importance of the *addition* of these books to the collection offered to students. Stoodt-Hill and Amspaugh-Corson (2001) remind educators that in creating a literacy experience that is well balanced, educators should consider "not only literary quality when selecting children's books, but also children's reading interests and issues as well" (p. 63).

Furthermore, providing access to books such as the four most commonly selected in this study, biographies of musicians, may increase students' nonfiction reading, particularly among girls who tend to select more fiction than nonfiction books (Doiron, 2003; Mohr, 2003; Simpson, 1996; Wiberg & Trost, 1970). Biographies of famous people may assist students in becoming more comfortable reading informational text and result in more nonfiction book selections.

3. Allow Time for Students to Build Reading Communities

Guice (1992) stated, "It is within the boundaries of communities that readers grow as readers" (p. 46). During the book fairs, participants formed reading communities around books, especially those reflective of media and mass marketing interests. Hepler and Hickman (1982) observed the impact of social interaction upon students' reading and also reported that a community of readers developed. In this study, it was common to hear in escalated voice levels, "Ohhh!!! Lil' Romeo! I'm getting this," and students quickly gathered around the book, *Pop People: Lil' Romeo* (Morreale, 2003). Students would share trivia about Lil' Romeo, the famous singer and actor, as they flipped through the book's contents. Overall, the reading communities that formed seemed to further stir students' interest in books.

Allow for students to talk about the books that they are selecting with one another during book selections. Knowing that a peer is interested in the same self-selected book and that a discussion may occur after reading the book can stimulate a student's interest in reading. If more than one copy of a desired book is available, two or more peers can read the same book and discuss its contents in literature circle format (Day, Spiegel, McLellan, & Brown, 2002).

4. Broaden Students' Familiarity with Books

In this study, books reflective of "kids' culture" were the most often selected and discussed among peers. One way to broaden students' familiarity with books is to use the impact of family members and teachers, as many participants of this study indicated that they influenced book selections. The below list includes specific strategies for broadening students' familiarity with books.

- Read aloud to students (an entire book or excerpts of books to stimulate interest); teachers, parents, and caregivers should be encouraged to read aloud a variety of genres and authors, including award-winning books, to model broadening familiarity with books (Hall & Williams, 2010).
- Teachers can provide book talks through YouTube or email before school begins and during holidays (such as the winter break) to encourage voluntary reading outside of school.

- Celebrate a book or two during a Book of the Month program at school where a book is publicized schoolwide by the principal. This celebration "blesses" a book and lets students know that the book must be good if the principal approves of it (Gambrell, 1996).

- When teachers individually confer with students regarding their book choices, they can gently direct students to select book topics, authors, series, and genres that have not been represented in their previous selections. For example, if a student has been reading a plethora of *Captain Underpants* books, the teacher might ask the student, "What else might interest you? Tell me about a place you might want to visit someday or an animal that you would love to know more about."

CONCLUSION

Research shows that successful readers read more than unsuccessful readers. In order to increase the likelihood that struggling readers will engage in voluntary reading, educators must provide access to books that are of interest. Studies that focus on book selections offer critical insight into reading material that may encourage voluntary reading. This book selection study revealed that participants chose books reflective of "kids' culture," particularly media and mass marketing interests.

Educators should consistently gain insight into "kids' culture," provide access to "kids' culture" books, and allow for time during school when students can create natural reading communities. Furthermore, educators, parents, and caregivers influence students' book selections, and these resources should be tapped as students broaden their familiarity with books.

REFERENCES

Allington, R. (2012). *What really matters in response to intervention: Research-based designs*, 3rd ed. Boston: PearsonAllynBacon.

Banks, C. (2003). *The History Channel presents the real Scorpion King*. New York: Scholastic Inc.

Day, J., Spiegel, D., McLellan, J., & Brown, V. (2002). *Moving forward with literature circles.* New York: Scholastic Inc.

Deci, E., & Ryan, R. (1985). *Intrinsic motivation and self-determination in human behavior.* New York: Plenum Press.

Doiron, R. (2003). Boy books, girl books. *Teacher Librarian, 30*(3), 14–18.

Fleener, C., Morrison, S., Linek, W., & Rasinski, T. (1997). Recreational reading choices: How do children select books? In W. M. Linek & E. G. Sturtevant (Eds.), *Exploring literacy* (pp. 75–84). Platteville, WI: College Reading Association.

Gambrell, L. (1996). Creating classroom cultures that foster motivation to read. *Reading Teacher, 50*(1), 4–25.

Glass, E. (2001). *Pop people: Destiny's Child.* New York: Scholastic Inc.

Guice, S. (1992). *Readers, texts, and contents in a sixth-grade community of readers.* Paper presented at the annual meeting of the National Reading Conference in San Antonio, Texas.

Hall, K., & Williams, L. (2010). First-grade teachers reading aloud Caldecott Award Winning books to diverse first-graders in urban classrooms. *Journal of Research in Childhood Education, 24,* 298–314.

Hepler, S., & Hickman, J. (1982). "The book was okay. I love you"—Social aspects of response to literature. *Theory Into Practice, 21*(4), 278–283.

Hunter, P. (2001). Raising children who want to read. Retrieved from http://www.libraryworks.com/LW_White%20Papers/pdfs/WP_Scholastic_1209.pdf

Johns, J., & Lenski, S. (2005). *Improving reading: Strategies and resources.* Dubuque, IA: Kendall Hunt Publishing Company.

Krashen, S. (2004). *The power of reading: Insights from the research* (2nd ed.). Portsmouth, NH: Heinemann and Westport.

Lamme, L. (1976). Are reading habits and abilities related? *Reading Teacher, 30*(1), 21–27.

McGill-Franzen, A. (1993). "I could read the words!": Selecting good books for inexperienced readers. *Reading Teacher, 46*(5), 424–426.

Medearis, A. (2002). *What did I do to deserve a sister like you?* New York: Scholastic Inc.

Mohr, K. (2003). Children's choices: A comparison of book preferences between Hispanic and non-Hispanic first-graders. *Reading Psychology, 24*(2), 163–176.

Morreale, M. (2003). *Pop people: Lil' Romeo.* New York: Scholastic Inc.

National Center for Education Statistics. (2010). *Fast facts.* Retrieved from http://nces.ed.gov/fastfacts/display.asp?id=147

Pilkey, D. (2001). *The Captain Underpants extra-crunchy book o' fun.* New York: Scholastic Inc.

Pilkey, D. (2002). *The all new Captain Underpants extra-crunchy book o' fun #2*. New York: Scholastic Inc.

Pilkey, D. (2003a). *Captain Underpants and the big, bad battle of the Bionic Booger Boy, Part 2: Revenge of the ridiculous robo-boogers*. New York: Scholastic Inc.

Pilkey, D. (2003b). *Captain Underpants and the big, bad battle of the Bionic Booger Boy, Part 1: The night of the nasty nostril nuggets*. New York: Scholastic Inc.

Pilkey, D., Beard, G., & Hutchins, H. (2002). *The adventures of Super Diaper Baby*. New York: Scholastic Inc.

Purves, A. C., & Beach, R. (1972). *Literature and the reader: Research in response to literature, reading interests, and the teaching of literature*. Urbana, IL: National Council of Teachers of English.

Scholastic Inc. (2003a). *How to draw Spider-Man*. New York: Scholastic Inc.

Scholastic Inc. (2003b). *Hangin' with Hilary Duff*. New York: Scholastic Inc.

Shannon, D. (1998). *A bad case of stripes*. New York: Scholastic Inc.

Simpson, A. (1996). Fictions and facts: An investigation of the reading practices of girls and boys. *English Education, 28*(4), 268–279.

Stoodt-Hill, B., & Amspaugh-Corson, L. (2001). *Children's literature: Discovery for a lifetime* (2nd ed.). Upper Saddle River, NJ: Prentice-Hall, Inc.

Turner, J. (1995). The influence of classroom contexts on young children's motivation for literacy. *Reading Research Quarterly, 30*(3), 410–441.

Walsh, K. (2002). *Hangin' with Lil' Romeo: Backstage pass*. New York: Scholastic Inc.

Wiberg, J., & Trost, M. (1970). A comparison between the content of first grade primers and the free choice library selections made by first grade students. *Elementary English, 48*, 792–798.

Williams, L. M. (2004). Helping students value the sole act of reading. *Dragon Lode, 22*(2), 29–33.

Williams, L. M. (2008). Book selections of economically disadvantaged Black elementary students. *Journal of Educational Research, 102*(1), 51–63.

Worthy, J., Moorman, M., & Turner, M. (1999). What Johnny likes to read is hard to find in schools. *Reading Research Quarterly, 34*(1), 12–27.

CHAPTER 5

Taking to the Streets!

One Principal's Path to Stemming Summer Reading Loss for Primary Grade Students from Low-Income Communities

Geraldine Melosh

SNAPSHOT

T IS AN early Thursday morning and the Florida sun has already promised to fulfill its late July potential as the thermometer attached to the side panel of the Summer Books! bookmobile—a 1999 white

Nissan four-cylinder pickup outfitted with a topper—reads 86 degrees. Mrs. Houston (all names are pseudonyms) parks the vehicle in the rutted, gravel driveway of Brandon Sweat's home in the western end of the county and lightly beeps the horn. She visits Brandon first each Thursday morning because, of all her students in the Summer Books! project, he lives in the most remote area of the county, about 7 miles northeast of State Road 20, along a labyrinth of dirt lanes. It is wise to visit Brandon in the mornings before Florida's notoriously violent afternoon storms make the washboard roads impassable to a vehicle such as the bookmobile.

Brandon (age 7), a mousy-haired boy with bright blue eyes, his brother Jeremy (age 6), and his sister Shalli (age 3) are waiting patiently on the metal steps of their grandmother's baby blue, single-wide trailer when Mrs. Houston arrives. Brandon holds a small, beige canvas bag filled with books and emblazoned with the words *Summer Books!* on his lap. All three children are barefoot, but appear freshly scrubbed. The boys wear matching Jaguar t-shirts and Shalli is dressed in a lightweight, sunflower-bedecked smock that reaches to her ankles. They live with their paternal grandmother, Mrs. Sweat, a thin, stooped woman in her late 50s who seldom smiles or talks during these visits. According to her, Brandon and Jeremy's mother abandoned them when they were toddlers, and their father—Mrs. Sweat's son—is in prison. Shalli, a half-sister, has lived with her grandmother since she was an infant. In all her summer visits, Mrs. Houston has never met or heard of an elder Mr. Sweat, and so assumes Mrs. Sweat is raising the children on her own, not an uncommon occurrence in this poor county.

To the right of the trailer is a broken-down metal swing set that has a knotted rope hanging from the top bar. There is a small, well-kept garden behind and to the left of the trailer that appears to be producing cherry tomatoes, okra, and summer squash in abundance. At Mrs. Houston's arrival, an old dog with arthritic joints slowly rises from his sandy bed under the trailer and saunters over to the bookmobile to be duly petted.

As soon as Mrs. Houston engages the emergency brake, Brandon, Jeremy, and Shalli run to greet her. They are young naturalists, every one of them, and insist that she come to the garden to see a praying mantis that they spotted earlier that morning. Like any 1st-grade teacher worth her salt, Mrs. Houston knows a lot about bugs and talks to them briefly about how important praying mantises are to gardeners. On the way back to the bookmobile, Brandon tells Mrs. Houston that he wants a book about praying mantises to read this week. Nature books, the Magic Tree House series by Mary Pope Osborne, and lately, the Bailey School Kids series by Dadey and Jones have been Brandon's top picks during Mrs. Houston's visits.

Back at the truck, Jeremy and Shalli know to keep themselves busy while Mrs. Houston spends a little time with Brandon. Mrs. Sweat watches from a distance, leaning against the door jamb of their trailer holding a mug of coffee and a cigarette. Using a survey downloaded onto her laptop, Mrs. Houston begins by asking Brandon to tell her what books he has read since their last visit. She asks how often, when, where, and with whom he has read the books and quickly enters the responses onto the laptop. She also asks him to tell her anything he especially liked (or didn't like) about the books he had selected. After a few minutes, she steps away from the bookmobile and addresses a few questions to Mrs. Sweat about how often her grandson read this week, if they talked about the books together at all, and if he had read with other family members or friends, again, entering the responses on her laptop. Next, she helps Brandon fill out the titles, dates, and authors for the books he read the preceding week on his "Books I Have Read" list so they can both keep track of the number of books he has read through the summer.

After completing the survey, Mrs. Houston asks Brandon to find a couple of pages in his favorite book and read them aloud to her. She notes the level of the book and does a quick running record of his reading to see that he is still selecting books fully within his instructional/ independent level. She collects the books, returns their cards to their slips, and returns the books to the bookmobile. While she does this, she tells Brandon to pick some new books (up to five) and directs him to the shelves within the bookmobile where he is most likely to find a "just right" book. Predictably, he picks a couple of nature books and two new Bailey School Kids books. Mrs. Houston also shows him a book she has found for him on salamanders (last week, the children had brought a captured lizard to her). She knows that this particular book is probably at Brandon's frustration level, but he is so enthralled with the topic, she believes he'll persevere in reading it. She apologizes for having no books on praying mantises, but promises to look for one for him for the next visit, a week away.

After Brandon checks out his five books and places them in his Summer Books! bag, Jeremy and Shalli are invited to pick out books for themselves. Mrs. Sweat is also invited to try to find a book to her liking in the adult, used-novel bin; she once again declines the offer. Jeremy, a 1st-grader, picks out a couple of level D books and Shalli finds a Disney picture book in the back of the bookmobile to "read." Mrs. Houston solicits a promise from Brandon and Jeremy to help Shalli with her book. Forty-two minutes after arriving, she gets a hug from the children and a brief wave from Mrs. Sweat and heads out to her next Summer Books! visit.

The preceding account describes an actual visit of a primary grade teacher in a makeshift bookmobile visiting a young boy at his home in rural Northeast Florida. The teacher was part of a University of Florida doctoral research project attempting to answer the question, "Can summer reading loss in high-poverty, primary-age children be reduced or reversed when they have the opportunity to regularly read books of interest to them during the summer break?" The question was not a purely academic one for the author of this article because, at the time, I was within 3 months of assuming a principalship at a small, high-poverty elementary school in a state that had not properly funded summer school programs for almost a decade.

The following sections of this chapter describe the Summer Book Project, its outcomes on the reading levels of high-poverty primary grade students, and some of the lessons learned and then applied in subsequent years as a principal and reading specialist in a Title 1 school.

SOCIOECONOMIC STATUS, STUDENT ACHIEVEMENT, AND SUMMER READING LOSS

Talk to almost any elementary teacher at the beginning of the school year and she or he will testify to the well-known phenomenon that the first several weeks of school are often devoted to playing catch-up with students to make up for the loss that they typically experience during the summer vacation break. Talk to primary grade teachers in schools serving high-poverty students and that observed phenomenon will be almost universal.

In the last 3 decades, there has been a growing consensus among many education researchers that summer vacations play a significant role in the seemingly intractable achievement gap that exists between poor and affluent students in the United States. Recently, a major newspaper (*The New York Times*) and magazine (*Time*) drew public attention to this phenomenon as well—a thing that educators have known intuitively and statistically for years.

Historically, school achievement has been studied in single snapshots as in cross-sectional studies (e.g., Coleman et al., 1966) or in longitudinal studies tied to an annual or biennial testing schedule (Juel, 1988). Yet increasingly, researchers recognize that both approaches miss the substantial seasonal variation in children's learning rates (Allington & McGill-Franzen, 2003; Entwisle, Alexander, & Olson, 1997; Ginsberg, Baker, Sweet, & Rosenthal, 1981; Heyns, 1978). Scores from tests given once a year give the distinct impression that high-socioeconomic children gain at a more rapid rate than low-socioeconomic children; that is, the latter derive less from school than the former.

However, when score gains are computed by season, separately for winter and summer, the data suggest that during the school year, all groups of children (regardless of their background characteristics) progress at approximately the same rate, but that there is a strong inverse relationship between the socioeconomic status of students and their summer achievement rates. Only during the summer do rates vary significantly; the pace of academic growth in poor children reflects the school calendar. This should not come as a big surprise. Unlike many families from low-socioeconomic levels, during the summer months, middle-class and more affluent families are more likely to take their children to museums and libraries, travel to distant places, and spend more hours per day reading (Entwistle et al., 1997). Middle-class parents have the resources to buy their children computers, age-appropriate books, and reading games; engage them more often in conversations using expansive vocabulary; and model reading as a form of enjoyment in their own lives (Baker, Gersten, & Keating, 2000).

Summer vacations appear to slow down or even reverse the achievement rates of some students and have minimal or even positive influence on the achievement rates of others. Perhaps the first researchers to formally recognize the differential impact of summer vacations on children of different socioeconomic backgrounds were Hayes and Grether (1983). They conducted an analysis of reading achievement and word knowledge scores for 370,000 2nd- through 6th-graders attending 600 New York City schools during the school year and the summer. They found overall gains in reading and vocabulary during the summer interval for the entire sample. However, when they disaggregated the data, schools enrolling many children from low-income families, and/or schools serving larger minority populations, showed average losses in reading and vocabulary while schools enrolling more affluent children showed gains. They felt justified in concluding that "in short, very little of the enormous difference in word knowledge performance appears to be attributable to what goes on in school; most of it comes from out of school . . . [and can] be accounted for by the differential effects of summer vacations" (p. 64).

Heyns's (1978) study of seasonal differences is probably the best known and the one that first explicated a conceptual framework for looking at seasonal differences in learning. Heyns compared children's academic growth when schools were open (fall and winter) to children's growth when schools were closed (summer). By doing this, she separated the effects of home background from the effects of school, for during the school year, both school and home can affect a child's growth, but in the summer, only home influences can affect their growth. Looking at the scores of thousands of 6th- and 7th-graders in Atlanta, she found that children's rates of gains made in the school year exceeded those made in the summer and that children's summer gains were inversely related to socioeconomic status. Family income is more highly related to summer gains or losses than to school year gains or losses.

Entwisle et al. (1997) reached a conclusion remarkably similar to Heyns's (1978) almost 2 decades later in their Baltimore School Study (BSS). The metaphor that these researchers used to describe this phenomenon was a *faucet*. The *faucet* is *on* during the school year for all children as they receive what they need to be able to progress satisfactorily, regardless of their background circumstances. However, during the summer months, the *faucet* is turned *off* for children from low-income families, who do not have the resources to keep them moving forward. By contrast, the *faucet* remains *on* during the summer for children from higher-income families, as these children continue to grow because their families and neighborhoods can supply them with resources needed to support their growth when school is not in session.

The good news of the results of these studies was that school effects are largely independent of social class and racial origins—contrary to what had become over time conventional educational wisdom (Coleman et al., 1966)—and that school effects have a substantial independent effect on the achievement of children. The bad news, of course, was that summer learning is considerably more dependent on parental status and that the gap between the richer and poorer students consistently widens over the summer.

Evidence then was mounting before this research was conducted that children from low-income families, on average, experience less reading achievement growth over the summer than do children from more affluent families. Children from these poorer families also have, on average, much less access to appropriate, well-matched books to read in their homes, daycare centers, and neighborhoods in the summer months, which may lead to less voluntary reading (Neuman & Celano, 2001) and voluntary reading has been associated with increased levels of reading achievement (Krashen, 2004). The literature strongly suggests that the summer reading loss in poor children may be directly linked to the differential access they have to appropriate reading materials outside of the school setting; however, the results of the few studies describing interventions that provide children with books during the summer are inconclusive (Paris, Pearson, Cervetti, Carpenter, Paris, DeGroot, & Mercer, 2004), suggesting that access to books is but one of several variables that affect the reading achievement of students during the summer vacation break.

The following describes one intervention that attempted to place appropriate books (i.e., books that children *could* read and would *want* to read) in the hands of a group of high-poverty 2nd-grade students via weekly bookmobile visits to their homes during the summer vacation break.

THE *SUMMER BOOKS!* PROJECT

Description

In this research project, 46 2nd-grade students from low-income families were randomly assigned to a treatment and control group. Students in the treatment group received weekly home visits from a teacher in a bookmobile for 10 weeks during the summer vacation. At each visit, children were allowed to select up to five books from a wide variety of topics and genres and given opportunities to talk about their books with the teacher. (Any interested family members were also allowed to select books during the visits, but were not considered part of the treatment group.) Students in the control group received no visits from the bookmobile, but were given books to take home at the end of the research project. In the spring before school was out, in the fall upon returning to school, and in the winter of their 3rd-grade year, students were assessed on measures of fluency, sight word knowledge, reading comprehension, and reading motivation.

Setting and Participants

The setting for this *Summer Books!* research was a poor, rural county located in Northeast Florida. Seventy-six percent of all elementary school children attending public school in this district at the time of the research received federal meal subsidies and every elementary school in the county was a Title 1 school. These conditions of poverty provided enormous challenges to the school district to educate every child well. At the time of the research, of the six surrounding counties, this one had the lowest reading scores at the 4th-, 8th-, and 10th-grade levels (Florida Department of Education, 2001).

Participants came from two Title 1 schools, one very rural and one located in the center of the county's seat. The percentage of students in the sample participating in the free/reduced-lunch program was 85%. By gender, the sample was pretty evenly distributed between boys (54%) and girls (46%). Ethnically and racially, the group broke down into African Americans (43%), Whites (50%), and Hispanics (7%). Based on the results of the state assessments, two-thirds of the children participating in the study were reading below grade level at the beginning of the project.

Summer Books! Bookmobile

Bookmobiles have a long and rich history in America (Wood, 1988). They have been, and still are, an extension of the services offered by conventional public libraries. They allow central public libraries to offer patrons in outlying areas and those who can't easily travel a quality of service they would not otherwise receive. The earliest bookmobiles were horse-drawn, coming into existence in the first decades of the 20th century. Motorized bookmobiles date from about the time of World War I.

The bookmobile used in the *Summer Books!* project consisted of a used pickup truck donated by a local doctors' organization and outfitted with a segmented topper similar to the ones subcontractors use to transport tools. Unlike modern library bookmobiles that are stocked on the inside with books and allow for entrance of children into the vehicle, but similar to the design of the original bookmobiles, this vehicle had side panels that opened parallel to the ground on either side, revealing shelves of books that could be reached from the outside of the truck. Children stood outside of the vehicle with the teacher to make their selections. There were also less accessible shelves of books in the bed of the truck that could be reached through the back doors.

Books

On its exterior side shelves, the *Summer Books!* bookmobile carried books ranging from preprimer to 5th grade (levels A through T) that were leveled according to Fountas and Pinnel's (1999) leveling system in genres that included fantasy, fairy tales, picture books, chapter books, biography, science, historical fiction, poetry, and plays. Fiction books outnumbered nonfiction books by a three-to-one ratio. The back of the truck held young adult novels, hi/lo selections, pulp fiction, preschool picture books, popular magazines for adults and teenagers, and local newspapers for family members to choose from. As the summer progressed, more books were added to the collection to accommodate students' interests (e.g., *Sunshine State Readers*, new *Harry Potter* books, and the *Magic Tree House* series). By the end of the summer, the bookmobile housed about 1,000 books. All books were paid for by a federal family literacy grant.

Procedures

The *Summer Books!* project lasted for 10 weeks—from the first week after the end of the school year in June to the week before the teachers returned for preplanning in August. Three weeks before the end of school, students were assessed on measures of reading fluency, comprehension, isolated sight word knowledge, and reading motivation. Upon completion of the assessments, students were randomly assigned from the two participating schools into the *Summer Books!* treatment group (N = 25) or the no-books control group (N = 21). Parents of children participating in the treatment group were called to arrange for a convenient time for weekly home visits and asked to send maps or detailed directions to their homes.

The bookmobile visits were shared between two primary grade teachers. One conducted visits Mondays, Tuesdays, and Wednesdays of each week; the other picked up the truck on Wednesday evenings and made visits on Thursdays and Fridays. Each child was scheduled to be visited once a week. Visits lasted between 15 and 45 minutes, depending upon the extended family participation. Teachers visited an average of five families a day.

During each visit, children were surveyed as to the amount of reading that had been done in the previous week and with whom the reading had been done. The teacher took a running record of the child reading from a couple of pages of the child's choice from a previous book. This allowed the teacher to chart the weekly progress of the student and determine what levels of books would be appropriate for selecting in the upcoming week. After the running record, children were directed to that portion of the bookmobile where he or she could pick "just right" books—ones that could be read with 90% accuracy or more, and those that were of personal interest to the child. Interested family members, including any adults in the family, were invited to select a book or magazine to check out once the child had made his or her selections.

SUMMARY OF FINDINGS

The results of this study were mixed. Overall, there were losses for the control group on all academic reading measures, thus supporting the literature on summer reading loss. There were losses and gains for students participating in the *Summer Books!* project, indicating that the intervention partially stemmed summer reading loss in the treatment group. There were no statistically significant differences on any measure or comparison of reading fluency or isolated sight word knowledge between the treatment and control groups. However, there were statistically significant differences between the treatment and control groups on one of the affective motivation measures (self-concept), due perhaps to students' ability to be able to select books of interest that were also at an appropriate reading level.

FIGURE 5.1. Mean gains and losses for full treatment and control groups on reading comprehension as expressed in lexiles at post-test.

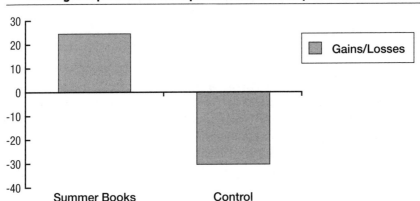

The most provocative finding came from the analysis of the scores in reading comprehension. At first blush, there were no statistically significant differences on any measure or comparison of reading comprehension between the treatment group as a whole and the control group. However, when the treatment group was parsed into those who had fully participated in the project (7 and 10 weeks of participation) and those who had only partially participated in the project (6 or fewer weeks) and then compared with the outcomes of the control group, a somewhat different picture emerged. Statistically analyzing the scores of only the *full* treatment group—who, on average, had read two and a half times more books during the summer than the *partial* treatment group—and the control group, there were differences in comprehension gain scores that approached statistical significance with the effect size for the treatment on this population in the moderate range (d = .54).

These results point to the possibility that for high-poverty children, the more intensive an intervention, the greater the impact on the reading achievement of children. That is, children, especially children from low socioeconomic levels, probably need to read much and often during the summer if maximum benefits are to be realized.

There was another finding that was important. As a group, children with histories of low achievement in reading (i.e., those who had been reading below grade level at pretest) who participated in this treatment had their summer reading loss stemmed and their scores showed the greatest absolute gains. However, this intervention did not improve the performance of these children enough to allow them to

FIGURE 5.2. Mean gains and losses for full treatment, partial treatment, and control groups on reading comprehension as expressed in lexiles at post-test. SB Full = those participating for 7–10 weeks. SB Partial = those participating for 6 weeks or fewer.

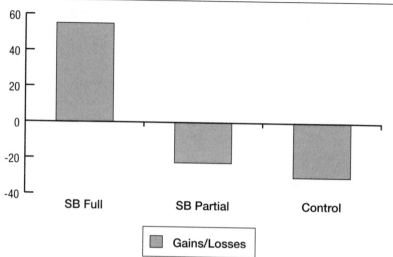

achieve grade-level reading scores at the end of the summer even when they had participated fully in the program. One conclusion that may be drawn from this is that although access to appropriate books is likely to stem summer reading loss for high-poverty primary-age students, access alone may not be sufficient to substantially improve outcomes in reading over the summer for students facing the double jeopardy of both low achievement histories and poverty.

However, this intervention—taking place with a small sample of students over only one summer vacation break—was, by design, limited in scope. Finding a substantial statistical effect with such a limited design promised to be problematic from the beginning. On the other hand, it is important to remember that a 1-month gain in reading for students during this intervention may actually represent a 3- to 4-month gain because the intervention eliminated a potential setback of 1 to 3 months.

Since this project was completed, other researchers, working with larger samples over multiple years, have found that placing a supply of self-selected trade books into the hands of high-poverty students during successive summer vacation breaks resulted in outcomes on state reading assessments that indicated a statistically significant effect (Allington, McGill-Franzen, Camilli, Williams, Graff, Zeig, Zmach, & Nowak, 2010).

THE PRACTICALITY OF A SUMMER BOOKS! PROGRAM

I consider myself to be primarily a practitioner, not an academician, though I hope my practice has been informed by the research of the latter cadre. As a former classroom teacher, school superintendent, director of a literacy nonprofit, reading specialist, and elementary principal, I have been trained to ask, "What works?" followed quickly by "Can we afford it?" Practicality, then, always consists of two elements: cost and effectiveness.

Cost

Over a decade ago, our state stopped funding elementary summer school programs as a categorical—that is, a category of expenditure with a dedicated funding source—and rolled it into the general operational funds of school districts. This, combined with the tightening of school budgets, resulted in a drastic reduction of educational opportunities provided for elementary students by schools during the summer months. If principals wanted to hold summer programs at their schools, they had to carve out dollars from their already overstretched school year budgets.

Was *Summer Books!* cost-effective? The cost of the research project was about one-third the cost of what it would have taken to run a traditional summer school program in this district for a comparable period of time. If one uses the number of all the school-aged children who received books through the project (i.e., family members of target children), the cost dropped to about one-fourth the cost of a traditional summer program. Thus, compared with typical summer school programs, it was cost-effective.

Effectiveness

Based on the outcomes of the research, a summer books–type project is a moderately effective intervention to stem summer reading loss in high-poverty children, especially for those *not* handicapped by histories of academic failure. However, the results of this research indicate that a weekly bookmobile intervention—even one as well crafted as *Summer Books!*—did not provide the intensity needed to substantially improve outcomes in reading over the summer for students who are poor *and* struggling.

The conclusion to be drawn from the results of this research is that for children doubly handicapped by poverty and low achievement, access to books during summer months was not sufficiently intense to move struggling readers forward enough to substantially narrow the gap between them and their more affluent classmates.

THE *JUMP AHEAD* PROGRAM:
SUMMER BOOKS!—THE NEXT GENERATION

In the intervening years since my research was completed, I have been a principal at a Title 1 elementary school in the district in which the research was conducted. Our school reflects the demographics of the rest of the community: Free and reduced-price lunch participation has hovered between 65% and 75% over the last decade, and ethnically and racially, our percentages mirror the county's: White (48%), African American (45%), Hispanic and other English Language Learners (7%). The teaching staff—a veteran group with an average of 13 years' experience among them—has successfully been running a summer books–type intervention since the summer of 2005. The intervention is called *Jump Ahead* and combines weekly bookmobile visits with school-based, intensive, one-on-one tutoring for our most struggling primary-age students—that is, those students who were determined to be reading below grade level at spring assessment and/or those students with histories of retention.

Program Description

Jump Ahead is comprised of two parts: The first is a one-on-one tutoring program that lasts for the first 3 weeks of the summer. It is conducted by highly qualified, primary grade teachers who have been trained in the reading strategies of Marie Clay's tutoring program, *Reading Recovery* (Clay, 1993). Sessions last 60 minutes a day and include the following components: 1) *Rereading of Familiar Books*: Students read and reread several familiar, leveled books ending with a running record on the previous day's new book. 2) *Working with Words*:

Students participate in a variety of interactive activities that build fluency with high-frequency words with phonics and phonemic awareness practice. 3) *Writing:* Using a *practice* and *perfect* page and Elkonin boxes, students work with their tutors to create an original sentence that culminates in cutting up and reassembling the sentence from a sentence strip. 4) *New Book*: Students are introduced to a new book (or portion of a longer book) each day where they are encouraged to apply strategies they have learned in prior lessons to reading the new print. A book is sent home each evening for students to read and reread to family members. Parents/guardians incur no cost, but transportation and lunch are not provided during these school-based sessions. At the end of the tutoring phase of *Jump Ahead*, participating children are sent home with a bag of high-interest books to keep. Book selections are based on the scores from their last running record assessment.

The 3 weeks of tutoring are followed by the second part of *Jump Ahead*—a summer books–type component where students are provided weekly visits to their homes via the school's bookmobile for the rest of the summer vacation break. Procedures followed during the visits are similar to procedures used during the *Summer Books!* research project.

Cost and Effectiveness of Jump Ahead

COST. By far, the largest cost involved in the *Jump Ahead* summer program is the cost of paying certified teachers to conduct tutoring for 3 weeks. However, for the last 4 years of the program, we have been successful in getting either Federal Programs (Title 1) or the Exceptional Student Education (ESE) Department to cover this cost. Title 1 understands this to be a program that provides supplemental intervention services for our *targeted assistance* population; ESE recognizes the program, rightfully, to be a means to reduce referrals and provide RtI (Response to Intervention) Tier III services.

In addition, several budget-friendly changes have been made to reduce the cost of the summer books portion of this intervention:

- Unlike the original *Summer Books!* project that used certified teachers to conduct the visits, we hire one full-time, well-trained paraprofessional to do the job at approximately 30% of the cost.
- Leveled books that now fill our school library and teacher resource center are used in the bookmobile, thus we incur no

additional book costs and we put into circulation books that would otherwise remain neglected and unused during the summer months.

- Although it is no longer pretty, we continue to use the same old pickup truck as our bookmobile. Our local friendly Firestone franchise continues to service it for free. The only cost associated with the vehicle is the purchase of gas, about $25 a week.

- A variety of administrative functions that support *Jump Ahead* (e.g., corresponding with parents, creating tutoring notebooks, training) are performed by our 12-month employees already on the payroll.

As long as the tutoring portion of *Jump Ahead* is paid for through other funding sources, the cost of running the 10-week program is approximately $100 a student. If the school must incur the cost of the tutoring as well, the cost increases to approximately $450 a student—still affordable, even in these days of tight budgets.

EFFECTIVENESS. No formal data have been kept since the inception of *Jump Ahead* specifically measuring the reading gains of *Jump Ahead* participants from May to August. Instead, *Jump Ahead* participants have been regularly assessed with their classmates on a variety of reading measures throughout the school years. As a result, no evaluation can be made of the short-term effectiveness of the *Jump Ahead* program that is not largely anecdotal.

However, the major concern with the summer reading loss phenomenon is the growing and accumulating achievement gap—at times estimated to be between 18 months and 3 grade levels in reading by the end of 5th grade (Allington & McGill-Franzen, 2003)—that occurs between different income groups as schooling progresses. Looking at the long-term effects of the intervention—that is, how students who were struggling as primary grade students performed on state exams at the end of their intermediate years—may provide more insight into its efficacy than looking at the short-term effects of the program.

To determine this, we looked at the 2010 Florida Comprehension Assessment Test (FCAT) scores for all 4th- and 5th-graders at our school who had participated in the *Jump Ahead* summer program at least once during their primary grade years. Bearing in mind that all of these students were reading *below* grade level in their early years of schooling, our findings were hopeful: Eighty-two percent of all former *Jump Ahead* participants (including special education students and second language learner students) scored at a proficient level in reading. Even more remarkable, of that group who passed the test, 33% passed with a score indicating that they were reading *above* the proficient level for their grade.

How much of this success in our intermediate students can be accounted for by participation in a comprehensive summer reading program during their primary grade years? It is impossible to determine with the data we have at hand, but the results are encouraging enough to warrant more research. We *do* know that all the children who participated in the *Jump Ahead* program were *targeted assistance* Title 1 students during their primary years. This means that they were low-income students targeted as being at-risk for school failure almost as soon as they walked through our doors. One foundational belief that guides our school is that reading problems need to be addressed early and intensively by highly trained professionals, and the more serious the problem, the more expert the help that is required to address the problem. All of these children received a multitude of instructional interventions during their school careers with us: high-quality classroom instruction that integrated reading and writing with the content areas from kindergarten onward; one-on-one kindergarten skills work; small-group, daily *push-in* tutoring groups; Saturday school; afterschool tutoring; parent involvement; and, of course, participation in our summer *Jump Ahead* program. It appears that the solid progress these students were able to make during the school year was sustained or even enhanced by the opportunity to participate in intensive instruction and regularly receive books of interest during the summer months.

CONCLUSION

Research indicates that children from low-income families experience summer reading loss without appropriate instructional interventions. The results of these *Summer Books!* projects support this conclusion. Research also indicates that children from low-income families do not all experience summer reading loss at the same rates, that is, lower-achieving poor children typically experience greater summer reading loss than higher-achieving poor children (Puma et al., 1997). The majority of the children who participated in *Summer Books!* were in double jeopardy—first by virtue of being poor, and second, by virtue of being low achievers. Although reading loss, on average, was stemmed in the children who participated, of those who were reading below grade level before the intervention began, only 5% made enough progress during the summer to progress to within the average band of reading achievement by 3rd grade. Thus, even though the effects of the intervention were significant, it was not powerful enough alone to narrow the widening gap that continues to exist between more and less affluent students.

However, the achievement of high-poverty, struggling students who have been given the opportunity to have regular access to appropriate reading materials *plus* opportunities for intensive instruction during the summer months of their primary years may be comparable to that of their more advantaged peers by the intermediate grades. By the time they are intermediate students, the achievement gap may not only be narrowed, but eliminated.

REFERENCES

Allington, R. L., & McGill-Franzen, A. (2003). The impact of summer loss on the reading achievement gap. *Phi Delta Kappan, 85*(1), 68–75.

Allington, R. L., McGill-Franzen, A., Camilli, G., Williams, L., Graff, J., Zeig, J., Zmach, C., & Nowak, R. (2010). Addressing summer reading setback among economically disadvantaged elementary students. *Reading Psychology, 31*(5), 411–427.

Baker, L., Gersten, R., & Keating, J. (2000). Why less may be more: A 2-year longitudinal evaluation of a volunteer tutoring program requiring minimal training. *Reading Research Quarterly, 35*(4), 494–519.

Clay, M. M. (1993). *An observational survey of early literacy achievement.* Auckland, NZ: Heinemann.

Coleman, J. S., Campbell, E. Q., Hobson, C. J., McPortland, J., Mood, A. M., Weinfeld, F. D., & York, R. C. (1966). *Equality of educational opportunity.* Washington, DC: U.S. Office of Education, National Center for Educational Statistics.

Entwisle, D., Alexander, K., & Olson, L. (1997). *Children, schools, and inequality.* Boulder, CO: Westview Press.

Florida Department of Education. (2001). *Statistical brief: Funding for Florida school districts.* Series 2000-01B. Tallahassee, FL: FLDOE.

Fountas, I. C., & Pinnell, G. S. (1999). *Matching books to readers*. Portsmouth, NH: Heinemann.

Ginsberg, A., Baker, K., Sweet, D., & Rosenthal, A. (1981, April). *Summer learning and the effects of schooling: A replication of Heyns*. Paper presented at the Annual Meeting of the American Educational Research Association, Los Angeles, CA.

Hayes, D. P., & Grether, J. (1983). The school year and vacations: When do students learn? *Cornell Journal of Social relations, 17*(1), 56–71.

Heyns, B. (1978). *Summer learning and the effects of schooling*. New York: Academy Press.

Juel, C. (1988). *Learning to read and write: A longitudinal study of fifty-four children from first through fourth grade*. Paper presented at the annual meeting of the American Education Research Association, New Orleans, LA.

Krashen, S. (2004). *The power of reading: Insights from the research* (2nd ed.). Portsmouth, NH: Heinemann.

McGill-Franzen, A., & Allington, R. (2003). Bridging the summer reading gap. *Instructor, 112 (8)*, 17-18.

Neuman, S., & Celano, D. (2001). Access to print in low-income and middle-income communities. *Reading Research Quarterly, 26*, 8–26.

Paris, S. G., Pearson, P. D., Cervetti, G., Carpenter, R., Paris, A., DeGroot, J., Mercer, M., et al (2004). Assessing the effectiveness of summer reading programs. In G. D. Borman, & M. Boulay (Eds.), *In Summer learning: Research, policies, and programs* (pp. 121–161). Mahwah NJ: Erlbaum.

Puma, M. J., Karweit, N., Price, C., Ricciuti, A., Thompson, W., & Vaden-Kienan, M. (1997). *Prospects: Final report of student outcomes*. (No. ED413-411). Washington, DC: U.S. Department of Education, Office of Planning and Evaluation Services.

Wood, D. (1988). A vehicle for outreach. *Wilson Library Bulletin, 45*(2), 45–46.

CHAPTER 6

Making Summer Reading Personal and Local

One District's Response

Lynn Bigelman

L IKE MANY OF my elementary principal colleagues, I begin preparing for the school year during the summer months. One of my many tasks is to create rich classrooms that are culturally, socially, and academically diverse. My focus is on exiting DRA (Developmental Reading Assessment) levels in order to establish academically heterogeneous classrooms. Prior to the first day of school, each teacher receives their class list with the most recent reading level assessed at the end of the previous school year. At this point in the year, I am

feeling pretty good about giving this information to my staff.

However, the truth be told, this elated feeling is relatively short-lived. It seemed in the past that only a couple of weeks into the school year, my teachers began questioning the reading level of many of their children. The child's current teacher would often question the integrity of the assessment, or worse, the former teacher's ability to administer the assessment accurately. Annually, these options put me into a tailspin and made me ponder the question: How could it be that the child lost so much between June and September? Where was the problem? Was it within us or was there something greater happening here that required our attention? What was the real issue?

Several years ago, I attended a session that Dick Allington and Anne McGill-Franzen gave, entitled "Summer Reading Loss," at the Michigan Reading Association annual conference. I was mesmerized . . . realizing that there was a real problem and it actually had a name. The issue was not the assessment process or the level of teacher expertise. The problem for many of our students is that reading activity is turned off during the 3-month summer break. Big ideas are forgotten, no more weekly trips to the library, and in many cases no more access to books at the students' independent level. Just as flowers need continuous care to flourish, so young readers grow when nourished by books. Our young readers do not require a great deal of luxury, but what they do need are educators who care enough about their learning to provide them with a supply of books to keep them growing.

SUMMER READING LOSS AS A LOCAL PROBLEM

Summer reading loss has the potential of becoming an enormous problem for kids if the current cycle is not broken (a loss of 3 months each summer accumulates to a gap of almost 2 years by the end of 6th grade). Thus, by middle school, summer reading loss, plus any initial achievement lag at the beginning of kindergarten, has produced a cumulative loss of 2 or more years in reading achievement.

Fortunately, several administrators from my district were also attending the conference. They either heard the same lecture or were willing for other reasons to address the problem. Together, we developed a plan. This plan would move us forward and would prove to curtail the amount of summer reading loss experienced by our students.

We began this journey 4 years ago. A group of principals and reading interventionists made preventing summer reading loss our primary initiative. Our district's principals, reading interventionists, special education teachers, and many entire building staffs had studied Allington's (2009) work with a concentration on *What Really Matters in Response to Intervention*.

Children's Interests

We understood the importance of putting high-interest, independent level books, in the hands of our children. Our first step, at every elementary building, was to create an interest survey for our students in the 1st grade. We began by asking for their book or topic preference (see Table 6.1).

After gathering this information and then generating the number of books needed at each independent level based on the DRA assessment, we realized that locating a funding source might be difficult. We also realized that spending the money on books for children had the potential of eliminating more funding for special services in the future. We were in the mindset of "pay now or pay later."

Funding Our Summer Books Program

Thus, a small group of principals and the supervisor of Elementary Education wrote a grant to the Waterford Foundation for Public Education to fund $16,375 for this endeavor. The Waterford Foundation for Public Education is an organization that supports teachers through individual donations from employees of the Waterford School District and others.

Each elementary principal also went to their school's PTAs or PTOs and asked for monetary support for this project. Miraculously, even during our troubled economic times in Michigan, we had secured enough money to begin our project.

Design of Our Summer Books Program

We started with all 1st-graders throughout our district involving 13 elementary schools and 832 students. We contacted several book vendors looking for the very best deal we could negotiate (including

TABLE 6.1. 1st-Grade Reading Interest Survey Results

DRA Text Level	0–4	6–8	10–12	14–16	18–28
Number of Students	94	130	136	187	285
Sports	XXX	XXX	XXX	XXX	XXX
Space			X	X	X
Volcanoes				X	X
Weather			X	X	X
Cartoon/TV	XXX	XXX	XXX	XXX	XXX
Math			X	X	X
Biographies			X	X	X
Animals/Dinosaurs	XXX	XXX	XXX	XXX	XXX
Henry and Mudge				XXX	XXX
Mystery	X	X	X	X	X
Biscuit			XXX		
Series				XXX	
Dr. Seuss			XX	X	X
Cars/Trucks	X	X	X		
Kevin Henkes				X	X
Berenstain Bears/ Arthur/Mo Willems			X	X	XXX

Note: X = amount of responses per category.

free shipping and books being leveled by their companies to expedite the process). Our goal was to put 20 or more books in the hands of our exiting 1st-graders.

Our orders were placed and filled, many boxes of books arrived, and our job was then to "prime the pump." The children at each elementary school had "shopping days" where they were able to select their own books at their independent reading level. Each school developed its own motivational tools to excite, entice, and encourage children to keep reading all summer long. Most schools planned for mid-summer meetings where children could exchange their recently read books for new books. Read-alouds were read by mystery readers—costumed adults, often school personnel—who read the books to kids.

And of course, children received treats and surprises to keep them reading. Some schools sent postcards home from teachers to encourage

FIGURE 6.1. Brownies and Books Event (Photo courtesy Jessica Keating)

You are invited to our **Brownies and Books Celebration!**
So bring your book bags to the Adams Library on July 15th
at 10:00 a.m. to exchange your summer books.

reading, while some students received phone messages, while others dialed into their teacher's school voicemail to hear a motivating message. Our summer reading project took on a life of its own, turning it into a community event.

Mid-summer reading reunions have become the norm in our community. Families, friends, neighbors, and teachers consider this our annual ritual. Many businesses have joined in a partnership with the schools to foster summer reading for our children. For example, Big Boy Restaurants sponsored our "Burgers and Books" during the summer. Children and parents received free burgers, fries, dinner coupons, and the live "Big Boy" (the principal in costume) at this event. Outback Restaurant encourages children to read "out back." Newspapers have covered these events and supported the local business partnerships:

G'Day Mate!
Hope you're having a BONZER summer. Be sure to make time for
summer fun and summer reading!
Remember to record the books you read in your
"Go OUTBACK and READ" book log, and be sure
to come out to the big . . .
Outback Book Exchange and Barbeque
at Riverside on Wednesday, July 22 between 4:30 and 6:00 p.m.

As students return in the fall, they are asked to return their summer reading books in their special bags (also a donation from State Farm insurance company). The vast majority of these books were

FIGURE 6.2. Waterford School District 2008 Summer Reading

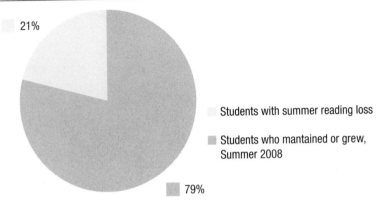

21%

Students with summer reading loss

Students who mantained or grew, Summer 2008

79%

returned in excellent condition. It was obvious that our children considered these books their treasures. Each child calculated the many minutes they spent reading that summer, which is part of our 1,000-minute reading challenge. Our librarians and reading interventionists helped make this a huge celebration, and our kids were the true beneficiaries.

OUTCOMES OF OUR SUMMER BOOKS PROGRAM

The reading interventionists have been responsible for assessing our students, relatively soon after school begins, in order to determine the results of our summer work. It was our mission that the majority of children would maintain their exiting grade reading level. Our district results demonstrated that by ensuring that children had access to books over the summer, almost 80% of our children maintained their reading level (see Figure 6.2).

We have now completed our fourth year of this project. We have secured additional funding through grants to add a grade level each year in our efforts to prevent summer reading loss. We currently serve grades 1–4. Our current 4th-graders were our first group to receive summer books in the 1st grade and have continued to receive them year after year. Figure 6.3 indicates that those students who received books for the last 3 years (current 4th-graders) have had the highest degree of success.

FIGURE 6.3. Adams Elementary 2009

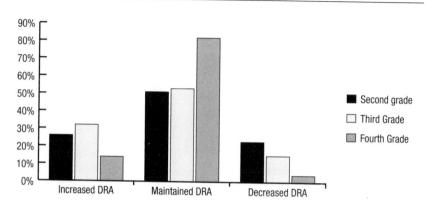

FIGURE 6.4. Special Education Students at Adams Elementary Reading Levels Fall 2010 (All students participated in Summer Reading Books)

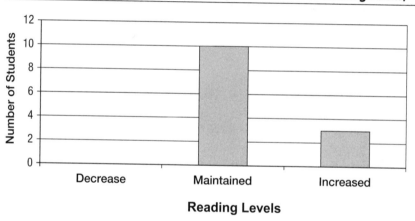

It is interesting to note that the success was especially impressive for our special education students, including students with learning disabilities, cognitive, and emotional impairments, as well as our students on the autistic spectrum. Therefore, even our most difficult to reach students have maintained or increased their reading levels by reading throughout the summer (see Figure 6.4).

Table 6.2 illustrates the funding sources we had to support the summer reading program. This year, we will continue our mission by requesting funding for our youngest children, our kindergartners.

TABLE 6.2. Summer Reading Program Funding Breakdown

Year	Waterford Foundation Grant	PTO/PTA
2007	$16,375	$100 x 13 schools
2008	$10,000	$100 x 13 schools
2009	$10,000	$100 x 13 schools
2010	$8,000	$100 x 13 schools
Subtotal	$44, 375	$5,200
Total:	$49,575	

In summary, our district is committed to preventing summer reading loss. In our community, everyone knows about the summer reading program. This has become the way we prepare for summer and the way our district supports our children through the summer months. Parents are educated on the importance of reading over the summer break and expect to see their children come home with a large bag of books on the last day of school. They look forward to the summer book exchange, which gets bigger and busier every year.

CONCLUSIONS

Our data demonstrate that students who read in the summer have the greatest degree of success in maintaining or increasing their reading achievement level. As we continue to build our summer library with the latest books, we will be able to give each child more books to take home over the summer. We will provide a bigger and better variety of student interest books and recruit more business partnerships to invest in the growth of our students during the summer. After 4 years of summer books, it is now hard to imagine that for so many years we didn't have this program. Our observed success ensures that our Summer Books project will continue in the future.

REFERENCE

Allington, R. (2009). *What really matters in response to intervention: Research-based designs.* New York: Pearson.

CHAPTER 7

Where Do We Go from Here?

Richard L. Allington
Anne McGill-Franzen

S TUDENTS' ENGAGEMENT IN reading practice is an important component of reading development (Krashen, 2011). Stanovich, West,
Cunningham, Cipielewski, and Siddiqui (1996) found that extensive
reading activity promoted growth on a wide range of academic measures. They found that better comprehenders read more voluntarily,
with this greater volume of reading producing greater vocabulary
growth, greater world knowledge, and greater knowledge of text struc-
tures. They pointed out that:

Thus, free-reading choices may explain part of the puzzle and the press-ing social problem of widening disparities between the educational haves and have nots. (p. 28)

In fact, the evidence provided in this book suggests that a major factor in the rich/poor reading achievement gap lies in the differences observed in the amount of voluntary summer reading done by students from families of different income levels. That consistent evidence ex-tends at least over the past 35 years (Alexander, Entwisle, & Olson, 2007; Cornelius & Semmel, 1982; Downey, Von Hipple, & Broh, 2004; Entwistle, Alexander, & Olson, 2001; Hayes & Grether, 1983; Heyns, 1978; Mraz & Rasinski, 2007; McCoach, O'Connell, Reis, & Levitt, 2006; Phillips & Chin, 2004), although much earlier reports noted the problem of summer reading loss, especially among children from low-income families (Aason, 1959; Elder, 1927). Given the broad concerns for narrowing rich/poor achievement, it seems critical that policy-makers and educators begin to better address the problem of summer reading loss. A good starting point would be addressing the problem of access to books that differentiates children living in more and less economically fortunate communities.

ACCESS TO BOOKS

As has been noted throughout this book, ease of access to books that students can read and books they want to read seems to deserve a cen-tral role in considering how best to address the problem of summer reading setback. Children from low-income families simply own far fewer books than do children from middle-income families, and they have more limited access to books in their schools and their commu-nities (Guice, Allington, Johnston, Baker, & Michelson, 1996; Heyns, 1978; Neuman & Celano, 2001; Phillips & Chin, 2004; Smith, Con-stantino, & Krashen, 1997). We know from an international study that children who grow up in homes with many books obtain 3 more years of schooling than children from largely bookless homes, independent of social class, parent education, and parent occupation. This advan-tage was twice as large as the difference between having a professional father versus having an unskilled laborer for a father. Growing up in a home where children had easy access to books also equaled the impact

Our summer books distribution work was found to provide "Near Top Tier" evidence of success in closing the rich/poor reading achievement gap. You can read the report on our study from the Coalition for Evidence-based Education in the Appendix at the end of this book. Additionally, our published paper on that study, "Addressing Summer Reading Setback among Economically Disadvantaged Elementary Students," that was published in the journal *Reading Psychology* in 2010, was identified by the International Reading Association as the recipient of the Albert J. Harris Award for 2012. This award is given annually to a published work that substantially contributes to the profession's understanding of reading/learning disabilities.

of having university educated parents versus unschooled parents (Evans, Kelley, Sikora, & Treiman, 2010). In other words, access to books is important regardless of family income, while at the same time access varies largely by family income.

We have now accumulated a number of experimental and quasi-experimental studies (Allington et al., 2010; Kim, 2004, 2006; Kim & Guryan, 2010; Kim & White, 2008) demonstrating that distributing books during the summer months can stem summer reading setback among children from low-income families and also improve measured reading achievement. Both outcomes narrow the existing reading achievement gap between children from low- and middle-income-level families.

In general, these studies demonstrate that providing relatively few books for summer reading will lead to most students engaging in voluntary summer reading. When voluntary summer reading occurs, we can expect to observe a small summer reading achievement growth and the elimination of summer reading setback (Allington et al., 2010; Lindsay, 2013). Given the relatively small cost (approximately $50 per student) of these summer books interventions, we find it surprising that so few school systems have adopted strategies for ensuring that all students, but especially students from economically disadvantaged homes, have access to books they can and want to read during the summer months. However, far too many of these same schools do not have well-stocked or staffed school libraries, do not have large classroom libraries, and do not participate in student book distributions during the school year. So, perhaps it is simply that most schools choose to ignore the substantial differences in access to books, but in doing so they seem to be fulfilling the long, sad story of low-income kids as struggling readers.

INNOVATIVE RESPONSES TO SUMMER READING LOSS

Many districts would cite insufficient funding for a free book distribution program such as we provided in our study, although we find many schools spend comparable amounts each year on test preparation materials and workbooks, neither of which have any evidence of improving reading achievement. We would suggest that schools consider loaning children's books from the school and classroom library collections over the summer to any child who is interested. Or the school library might open 1 day each week over the summer to provide children access to those books. But there are other options that schools should also consider.

For instance, Malach and Rutter (2003) report on a summer reading project focused on transitioning 1st-graders that was similar in some ways to the effort described by Geri Melosh in Chapter 5. The school outfitted an RV as a mobile tutoring center. Five target urban neighborhoods were identified and the RV began weekly neighborhood visits in mid-June and continued through mid-August. Three teachers offered one-to-one or small-group lessons to any child who visited the RV each week and also monitored student book exchanges. Any elementary child could visit for books, but transitioning 1st-graders got the reading lessons. Assessments demonstrated that 76% of participating children maintained or improved upon their spring reading level.

Willman (1999) asked children to call her school voicemail and either read to her for 3 minutes or summarize a chapter of the book they were reading. She received 92 calls from 26 children over the summer months. None of the children who called experienced a decline in reading performance as a result of summer vacation.

We could also create summer school programs that target increasing reading volume substantially. This is something that few summer school programs manage to accomplish. However, Shin (2001) reports on a quasi-experimental study examining the impact of a 6-week self-selected reading initiative on 200 6th- and 7th-graders attending summer school because of poor reading achievement. This program ran 4 hours daily, with approximately 2 hours devoted to self-selected sustained silent reading. An investment of $25 per student in popular series titles and magazines created the large supply of interesting texts that students chose for their own reading. In addition, 45 minutes each day were spent in reading and discussion of award-winning novels such as *Island of the Blue Dolphins* and *Where the Red Fern Grows*. Control group students (n = 160) were given no books or special materials but used the curriculum materials typically used in the district's language arts classes. There was a significant difference in gains, favoring the experimental students on the ALTOS reading test (a gain of about 5 months for experimental subjects) and the experimental subjects gained 1.4 months on the comprehension section of the Nelson-Denny Reading Test.

Likewise, McGill-Franzen and Love-Zeig (2008) report on a summer school project where text sets on bugs or sea life were created as the focus for the daily 30- to 60-minute Summer Reading Club. They describe how the primary grade children used illustrations (cutaway drawings, timelines, lists) to support their learning from multiple texts on a topic. Participants in the Summer Reading Club had greater reading gains than children in the control group that also did summer school but without the Summer Reading Club activities.

There are obviously many other strategies that schools might use to put books in the hands of poor children during the summer months. If a summer school program, for instance, serves only some children, perhaps procedures that might include school buses for regular bus routes, family notification, early morning and evening hours as well as regular school hours on the designated day, could be developed to allow other children to visit school weekly to select summer books from the school library to read and perhaps discuss the book they read with a teacher, paraprofessional, young adult volunteer, or with other children.

Some local public libraries have historically organized summer reading events. Schools might partner by sending reading recommendations for library postings or paying for weekly or bimonthly days when teachers might be available to discuss books with students at the library if opening the school for this purpose is not possible. However, for a number of reasons low-income families make less use of public libraries than do more economically advantaged families. Public libraries must reach out to less economically advantaged parents and children in order to play an increasingly larger role in providing these families with access to books for summer reading.

Currently, middle-class children are more likely to be engaged in organized summer programs than children from low-income families.

In a recent review funded by the Wallace Foundation of the effectiveness of summer programs at improving the academic and social well-
being of children, the authors report that:

> Participation varied among participants who differed with respect
> to family structure and economic backgrounds ($p<.001$). Children
> who participated in summer programs were more likely to: reside
> in households with two biological or adoptive parents (28 percent
> versus 21 percent of those who reside with single mothers); and
> come from higher-income households that are at least 200 percent
> above of the poverty line (29 percent versus 18 percent for those
> from lower income households). However, after controlling for the
> covariates (i.e., gender, race, poverty, and family structure) socio-
> economic differences were the only differences that remained. The
> strong association between poverty and program participation is
> consistent with research on out-of-school time programming which
> has found that children living in families below 200% of the federal
> poverty line are less likely to participate in activities out of school
> (34 percent compared with 9 percent) than children from more
> economically advantaged families. (Terzian, Moore, & Hamilton,
> 2009, p. 7)

CONCERNS ABOUT ADDRESSING SUMMER READING SETBACK

The research completed to date suggests an important role for at least
considering a student's interest when selecting books for summer
reading (see Chapter 2). Some studies demonstrating improved reading
achievement during the summers have allowed students to self-select
the titles they wanted from a summer book fair, as we did in our study
(Allington et al., 2010). Other studies gathered data on topics students
were interested in before the summer began and then used that information to select books for each 4th-grade student's summer reading
(Kim, 2006). In this single year study, the effects of the free books distribution on reading achievement was significant for Black and Hispanic students, but not for Caucasian students. The largest positive
effects on reading achievement were observed for students who had
reading levels below their grade level and students who owned the few-

est books. These findings make sense in that struggling readers are the children most likely to experience summer reading setback, alongside children who are poor and have limited access to books to read during the summer.

What no one has managed to do is demonstrate that reading a required list of summer books raises reading achievement, though many school districts have such summer reading requirements, at least for the higher-achieving students. However, Kim (2004) examined the effects of reading from a district-provided summer reading list for 6th-grade students. This list noted 130 different books that students might read over the summer. He notes that only a minority of the students actually read the five self-selected titles that were expected, while a substantially larger number of students report reading no books during the summer than reading the five books expected by the school district. However, what Kim did note was that actually reading five books during the summer months stemmed summer reading loss. Here again, though, students self-selected the books they read during the summer months, though from the list of 130 titles offered by the district. In addition, if the school district had provided copies of the books the students read, then, perhaps, more students would have completed the readings and earned the benefit of improved reading proficiency. Actually providing the books, not just a list of possible books, removes the access problem that a list creates, since parents will still have to take their children to a bookstore or a library to locate the books the child wants to read from the list. Although a trip to either a library or a bookstore may seem to be an insignificant obstacle, the vast majority of students in Kim's study never read the five books recommended, suggesting the families involved perceived either option as an obstacle.

Kim and Guryan (2010) report on a summer books study that produced no reading growth. However, this study was but a single-year intervention and although the 400 intermediate grade Hispanic students self-selected their books, they typically selected books that had readability levels above their reading levels, which may be the reason for the disappointing outcome that found no significant difference in the reading achievement of students who participated in the summer books project and students who did not and served as the control group. However, the students in the summer books group did improve their oral reading fluency performance over the summer while the control group students had no such improvement. The authors note several explanations for the lack of effects on broad measures of reading achievement, including that while volume of reading increased it did not increase by a large amount.

Two Issues to Begin with

These studies demonstrate two issues of concern: 1) How important is self-selection of books to be read? and 2) How important is text complexity in summer voluntary reading?

SELF-SELECTION. In the study we conducted (Allington, McGill-Franzen et al., 2010), we privileged self-selection and largely ignored text difficulty except that we selected the 400 to 500 titles from which students self-selected their books. When we selected the titles each year, we tried to ensure that all participants would be able to locate books at their reading levels. In addition, because so many of the participants in our study were reading below grade level, we always had a large number of "easy" books students could select from. Still, we were troubled that too many of the weakest readers in our study selected books that were several levels above their reading level, books they could not read (as a sample demonstrated when we asked them to read aloud from these books). It was the weakest readers in our study who were least likely to benefit much from our summer books distribution, perhaps because they seemed unable to self-select books of an appropriate level of complexity.

A similar pattern on a somewhat larger scale was reported by Kim and Guryan (2010), who noted that they felt a primary reason their summer book distribution produced no positive effects on reading achievement compared with the control group was that two-thirds of the intermediate grade students in their study selected books above their reading levels, suggesting that most students selected books they could not actually read.

We noted what we termed a "social bias" effect in the book selections of struggling readers. The social bias was that struggling readers often followed the better readers around and selected the same books the better readers selected. This often meant that students who should have been selecting a *Junie B. Jones* series book instead selected a *Harry Potter* series book. They selected the *Harry Potter* book because that was a book selected by their better-reading peers.

In addition, it also became clear that many struggling readers had developed few skills in selecting books they could read accurately. We had some of our students read aloud from their self-selected texts for a minute or 2. Too often, it was painfully apparent that the book they had selected was far too difficult. In many cases, after a few unknown words were encountered, the student would ask us whether they could swap that book for a different one (see Williams, Chapter 4, this book for more details on book selection). We allowed them, in these cases, to return to the book fair and select a different title. In our study, then, we observed that many struggling readers had difficulty selecting books they could actually read. Perhaps it was more than simple social bias, though, that led them to select books they could not read. Our observations indicated that far too many struggling readers selected books based on the cover art and rarely, if ever, attempted to read the text or even read the back cover copy that every book displayed. In short, we had a sense that most struggling readers were largely inexperienced at self-selecting texts to read.

This suggests that schools might provide all students with good guidelines for book selection. These might be provided by the school librarian or alternatively by the classroom teacher. They could be fairly simple and might include having the teacher introduce book selection by pointing out these possible steps in selecting the right book:

1. Turn the book over and look at the back cover. In many cases, the back cover has a brief introduction to the book. Read it and see if you still think you will want to read the book.
2. If you still think you want this book, then open the book to almost any page. Now read the page to yourself. If you find more than one or two words on the page that you cannot read, you probably will find the book difficult and you may never finish it. If the book is too hard, look for another book and do these same two steps until you find a book you can read and want to read.
3. The teacher might model her own self-selection of a book using a think-aloud approach while deciding among several books.

Additionally, providing greater opportunities for self-selection of books during the regularly scheduled reading class periods and ensuring the self-selected books are available for voluntary reading at home during the school year would create many opportunities for evaluating the skill all readers have in self-selecting appropriate books for personal reading and for coaching improved self-selection practices, while not discouraging the pleasure and autonomy of self-selection.

When it comes to engaging children in voluntary reading over the summer months, self-selection becomes of paramount importance. At the same time, self-selection can be considered broadly (selecting a book from a library collection or from the collection available at a large bookstore) or more narrowly (selecting from three choices provided by the teacher or selecting from a small classroom library). We don't have much in the way of research on how many book titles and levels of books make an adequate base for satisfying the power that self-selection has exhibited in the meta-analyses done by John Guthrie and Nicole Humenick (2004) and James Lindsay (Chapter 2). What we do know, based upon their meta-analyses is that increasing access to texts students consider interesting and providing for self-selection both produced a positive effect on reading comprehension that was 10 times larger than the effect on reading comprehension that was reported by the National Reading Panel (2001) for providing explicit phonics instruction.

TEXT COMPLEXITY. When it comes to a question of appropriate levels of text complexity for summer voluntary reading, there is little to suggest recommending difficult texts. This is an issue, however, since we get far more calls each year from parents wondering whether we have a list of "difficult" books that would be appropriate their child. We always tell these parents that we do have some difficult books that they could read, but that children need books they can read accurately, fluently, and with 90% comprehension. This is what was labeled the "independent reading level" by Emmett Betts back in the 1940s. Since his original analysis, a number of studies have verified the need for students to experience this sort of "high success reading" (c.f., Berliner, 1981; Ehri, Dreyer, Flugman, & Gross, 2007; Gambrell, Wilson, & Gantt, 1981; O'Connor, Bell, Harty, Larkin, Sackor, & Zigmond, 2002). One could argue that one reason too many students struggle as readers is that too many students have desks and backpacks filled with books they cannot read accurately and independently.

It should surprise no one that our struggling readers exhibit lower levels of motivation for reading and lower levels of engagement in

Choice of Books to Read During the Summer Is Controversial

Our summer books study was discussed in several popular media outlets (*New York Times, USA Today*) and was the subject of a *New York Times* online blog. The blogger, Tara Parker-Pope, wrote,

> One of the most notable findings was that children improved their reading scores even though they typically weren't selecting the curriculum books or classics that teachers normally assigned for summer reading. That conclusion confirms other studies suggesting that children learn best when they are allowed to select their own books.

Parker-Pope also interviewed study co-author Anne McGill-Franzen about the book choices children made in the study. Reader response was rapid and voluminous! Some respondents argued for having their children read award-winning titles and classic children's literature during the summer, while others wrote gratefully of growing up in homes where what they read during the summer months was largely left up to them. What was obvious in reading the pages of responses was that summer reading is a topic readers of the *New York Times* are familiar with and engaged in. You can read the blog entry and the responses at http://well.blogs.nytimes.com/2010/08/02/summer-must-read-for-kids-any-book/?emc=eta1.

reading. Faced with a steady supply of too-difficult books, struggling readers often just give up (Allington, 2002). In addition, they begin to see themselves as failures—literacy failures—and humans rarely voluntarily engage with activities they see themselves as failures in. If we hope to attract students to engage in voluntary reading, and especially voluntary summer vacation reading, then we must work to ensure that every potential summer reader will be able to locate many books he can read and books he will want to read voluntarily.

A Third and Final Issue: Assessment of Educational Effects

Evaluating whether a summer voluntary reading program has an impact on reading achievement is messy business—messy because we could measure small things such as improvements in reading rate (often mislabeled fluency) or large things such as improvement in the comprehension of texts read. However, no matter what we decide to measure, we are left with assessment tools that yet leave much to be desired. The reading rate measures most often used (e.g., DIBELS) are short, especially written grade-level passages that students read aloud when what we really need are measures of reading rate across longer segments of authentic text read silently. Reading comprehension assessments (e.g., Gates-MacGinite Reading Test, Woodcock Reading Mastery Test) typically used multiple-choice questions or modified cloze replacement strategies for assessing recall of short texts (with the text still there in front of the reader), when what we really need are essay responses to silently read, complete texts. In other words, what we really want to assess is rarely what we can assess given modern reading assessments.

In addition to these limitations, current assessments are not very reliable at estimating individual reading achievement nor at measuring reading growth over very short periods of time. These two limitations are related. During the typical summer school vacation period, it has been estimated that middle-class children add about 1 month's reading growth (Cooper, Nye, Charlton, Lindsay, & Greathouse, 1996). However, the standard error of measurement on virtually all reading assessments is far larger than this very small amount of expected growth. It is this latter factor that led us (Allington et al., 2010) to conduct a 3-year-long longitudinal study of the effects of free, voluntary summer reading. Our assumption was that after three consecutive summers, the amount of potential growth we might expect to observe should be large enough to capture on a commercial reading achievement test. We were correct in that assumption and will suggest that at least some of the shorter-term studies (c.f., single-year studies) of summer voluntary reading might have reported not obtaining statistically significant effects on reading achievement as much because of measurement problems of this sort.

School officials must consider this fundamental problem in evaluating the effects of summer educational efforts, including both summer school effects and the effects of voluntary summer reading programs (Paris, Pearson, Cervetti, Carpenter, Paris, DeGroot et al., 2004). The future may bring us assessment tools that both measure what we want to measure and measure even small amounts of growth accurately. But the future is not here yet, and so evaluation of summer reading efforts must be undertaken with care.

CONCLUSION

Ensuring that every child has books to read over the summer is but one step to addressing the rich/poor reading achievement gap. Many children will need more than voluntary summer practice to ensure that they develop high levels of reading proficiency. However, the evidence on the role of summer reading loss in extending the achievement gap has been ignored for far too long. Likewise, the evidence of the limited access that poor children have to books (or magazines or newspapers) has been too long ignored. It doesn't seem likely that the achievement gap can be narrowed without efforts that focus on out-of-school factors, with voluntary reading a critical factor to focus on. Alexander, Entwisle, and Olson (2001) argued that:

> Schools do matter, and they matter most when support for academic learning outside school is weak. School-based public resources do not completely offset the many and varied advantages that accrue to children of privilege by virtue of private family resources outside school. (p. 183)

We are a rich enough nation to ensure that any child who wants a book to read will have a book to read on any given day of the week, regardless of whether school is in session or not. When compared with the costs of many popular interventions, providing poor children with access to a rich and engaging supply of books is inexpensive. Talk of a "right to read" is premature if books are largely out of reach for poor children and their parents (McGill-Franzen & Allington, 1993).

We can continue to bemoan the rich/poor reading achievement gap while doing little productively to narrow that gap. Alternatively, we could become actively engaged in using what we've learned about the power of free, voluntary reading to begin to address the achievement gap. One of the proven strategies for narrowing the achievement gap is to focus on summer reading activity. Research has consistently demonstrated that children from low-income families read far less every summer than do children from middle-income families. Research has demonstrated that one primary reason that poor children do not read during the summer months is their limited access to books in their homes, in their schools, and in their neighborhoods (Neuman & Celano, 2001). Research has also shown that simply providing books matched well to children's reading levels and their interests improves reading achievement and, in fact, largely eliminates summer reading loss, thereby narrowing the rich/poor reading achievement gap.

We are now at the point where educators and education policymakers must decide whether to continue to ignore what the research has shown or to act upon those findings. In the end, we must remember that this is a choice adults must make, but it is our children who will either benefit or pay the price based on what we choose to do. If having a sizable impact on the achievement gap was an expensive proposition, then we could understand a reluctance to move ahead, but when the cost is very modest, roughly the cost of three commercial workbooks or $50, then failing to move ahead seems almost criminal.

So let's end with a question: Will we choose to address narrowing the reading achievement gap by providing kids with books to read during the summers, or will we continue to do largely nothing in this regard? The kids are waiting for the answer.

REFERENCES

Aason, H. (1959). A summer's growth in reading. *Elementary School Journal, 60*(1), 70–74.

Alexander, K. L., Entwisle, D. R., & Olson, L. S. (2001). Schools, achievement, and inequality: A seasonal perspective. *Educational Evaluation and Policy Analysis, 23*(2), 171–191.

Alexander, K. L., Entwisle, D. R., & Olson, L. S. (2007). Lasting consequences of the summer learning gap. *American Sociological Review, 72*(2), 167–180.

Allington, R. L. (2002). You can't learn much from books you can't read. *Educational Leadership, 60*(3), 16–19.

Allington, R. L. (2012). *What really matters for struggling readers: Designing research-based programs*, 3rd ed. Boston: Pearson-Allyn-Bacon.

Allington, R. L., McGill-Franzen, A. M., Camilli, G., Williams, L., Graff, J., Zeig, J., Zmach, C., & Nowak, R. (2010). Addressing summer reading setback among economically disadvantaged elementary students. *Reading Psychology, 31*(5), 411–427.

Berliner, D. C. (1981). Academic learning time and reading achievement. In J. Guthrie (Ed.), *Comprehension and teaching: Research reviews* (pp. 203–225). Newark, DE: International Reading Association.

Cooper, H., Nye, B., Charlton, K., Lindsay, J., & Greathouse, S. (1996). The effects of summer vacation on achievement test scores: A narrative and meta-analytic review. *Review of Educational Research, 66*, 227–268.

Cornelius, P. L., & Semmel, M. I. (1982). Effects of summer instruction on reading achievement regression of reading disabled students. *Journal of Learning Disabilities, 15*(7), 409–413.

Downey, D. B., von Hippel, P. T., & Broh, B. A. (2004). Are schools the great equalizer? Cognitive inequality during the summer months and the school year. *American Sociological Review, 69*, 613–635.

Ehri, L. C., Dreyer, L. G., Flugman, B., & Gross, A. (2007). Reading Rescue: An effective tutoring intervention model for language minority students who are struggling readers in first grade. *American Educational Research Journal, 44*(2), 414–448.

Elder, H. E. (1927). The effect of summer vacation on silent reading ability in the intermediate grades. *Elementary School Journal, 27*, 541– 546.

Entwisle, D. R., Alexander, K. L., & Olson, L. S. (2001). Keep the faucet flowing: Summer learning and home environment. *American Education, 25*(3), 11–15 & 47.

Evans, M. D. R., Kelley, J., Sikora, J., & Treiman, D. J. (2010). Family scholarly culture and educational success: Books and schooling in 27 nations. *Research in Social Stratification and Mobility, 28*(2), 171–197.

Gambrell, L. B., Wilson, R. M., & Gantt, W. N. (1981). Classroom observations of task-attending behaviors of good and poor readers. *Journal of Educational Research, 74*(6), 400–404.

Guice, S., Allington, R. L., Johnston, P., Baker, K., & Michelson, N. (1996). Access? Books, children, and literature-based curriculum in schools. *The New Advocate, 9*, 197–207.

Guthrie, J. T., & Humenick, N. M. (2004). Motivating students to read: Evidence for classroom practices that increase motivation and achievement. In P. McCardle & V. Chhabra (Eds.), *The voice of evidence in reading research.* (pp. 329–354). Baltimore: Paul Brookes Publishing.

Hayes, D. P., & Grether, J. (1983). The school year and vacations: When do students learn? *Cornell Journal of Social Relations, 17*, 56–71.

Heyns, B. (1978). *Summer learning and the effects of schooling.* New York: Academic Press.

Kim, J. (2004). Summer reading and the ethnic achievement gap. *Journal of Education of Students at Risk, 9*, 169–189.

Kim, J. S. (2006). Effects of a voluntary summer reading intervention on reading achievement: Results from a randomized field trial. *Educational Evaluation and Policy Analysis, 28*(4), 335–355.

Kim, J. S., & Guryan, J. (2010). The efficacy of a voluntary summer book reading intervention for low-income Latino children from language minority families. *Journal of Educational Psychology, 102*(1), 20–31.

Kim, J. S., & White, T. G. (2008). Scaffolding voluntary summer reading for children in grades 3 to 5: An experimental study. *Scientific Studies of Reading, 12*(1), 1–23.

Krashen, S. (2011). *Free voluntary reading.* Santa Barbara, CA: Libraries Unlimited.

Lindsay, J. J. (2013). Impacts of interventions that increase children's access to print material. In R. L. Allington & A. McGill-Franzen (Eds.), *Summer reading: Closing the rich/poor reading achievement gap.* New York: Teachers College Press.

Malach, D. A., & Rutter, R. A. (2003). For nine months kids go to school, but in summer this school goes to kids. *Reading Teacher, 57,* 50–54.

McCoach, D. B., O'Connell, A. A., Reis, S. M., & Levitt, H. A. (2006). Growing readers: A hierarchical linear model of children's reading growth during the first 2 years of school. *Journal of Educational Psychology, 98*(1), 14–28.

McGill-Franzen, A. M., & Allington, R. L. (1993, October 13). What are they to read? Not all kids, Mr. Riley, Have easy access to books. *Education Week,* 26.

McGill-Franzen, A. M. , & Love-Zeig, J. (2008). Drawing to learn: Visual support for developing reading, writing, and concepts for children at risk. In J. Flood, S. B. Heath, & D. Lapp (Eds.), *Handbook of research on teaching literacy through the communicative and visual arts* (Vol. II, pp. 399–411). New York: Lawrence Erlbaum Associates.

Mraz, M., & Rasinski, T. V. (2007). Summer reading loss. *Reading Teacher, 60*(8), 784–789.

National Reading Panel. (2001. *Teaching children to read: An evidence-based assessment of the scientific research literature on reading and its implications for reading instruction.* Retrieved from http://www.nationalreadingpanel.org

Neuman, S., & Celano, D. (2001). Access to print in low-income and middle-income communities. *Reading Research Quarterly, 36,* 8–26.

Paris, S. G., Pearson, P. D., Cervetti, G., Carpenter, R., Paris, A. H., DeGroot, J., et al. (2004). Assessing the effectiveness of summer reading programs. In G. D. Borman & M. Boulay (Eds.), *Summer learning: Research, policies, and programs* (pp. 121–161). Mahwah, NJ: Lawrence Erlbaum Associates.

O'Connor, R. E., Bell, K. M., Harty, K. R., Larkin, L. K., Sackor, S. M., & Zigmond, N. (2002). Teaching reading to poor readers in the intermediate grades: A comparison of text difficulty. *Journal of Educational Psychology, 94*(3), 474–485.

Phillips, M., & Chin, T. (2004). How families, children and teachers contribute to summer learning and loss. In G. D. Borman & M. Boulay (Eds.), *Summer learning: Research, policies and programs* (pp. 255–278). Mahwah, NJ: Lawrence Erlbaum.

Shin, F. H. (2001). Motivating students with *Goosebumps* and other popular books. *California School Library Association Journal, 25*(1), 15–19.

Smith, C., Constantino, R., & Krashen, S. (1997). Differences in print environment: Children in Beverly Hills, Compton and Watts. *Emergency Librarian, 24,* 8–9.

Stanovich, K. E., West, R. F., Cunningham, A. E., Cipielewski, J., & Siddiqui, S. (1996). The role of inadequate print exposure as a determinate of reading comprehension problems. In C. Cornoldi & J. Oakhill (Eds.), *Reading comprehension difficulties: Processes and intervention* (pp. 15–32). Mahwah, NJ: Lawrence Erlbaum Associates.

Terzian, M. A, Moore, M. K., & Hamilton, K. (2009). *Effective and promising summer learning programs and approaches for economically–disadvantaged children and youth.* Washington, DC: Child Trends, The Wallace Foundation.

Willman, A. T. (1999). "Hello, Mrs. Williams, it's me!" Keeping kids reading over the summer by using voice mail. *Reading Teacher, 52,* 788–789.

Evidence Summary for Annual Book Fairs in High-Poverty Elementary Schools

From Coalition for Evidence-Based Policy, a nonprofit, nonpartisan organization.

Main study

Allington, Richard L., Anne McGill-Franzen, Gregory Camilli, Lunetta Williams, Jennifer Graff, Jacqueline Zeig, Courtney Zmach, and Rhonda Nowak. "Addressing Summer Reading Setback Among Economically Disadvantaged Elementary Students." *Reading Psychology*, 2010, vol. 31, no. 5, pp. 411–427.

Highlights

INTERVENTION: Annual book fairs to provide summer reading to students in high-poverty elementary schools over 3 years, starting at the end of 1st or 2nd grade

EVALUATION METHODS: A well-conducted randomized controlled trial

KEY FINDINGS: Increase in students' reading achievement by 35–40% of a grade level, 3 years after random assignment

OTHER: A study limitation is that its sample was geographically concentrated in two Florida school districts. Replication of these findings in a second trial, in another setting, would be desirable to confirm the intervention's effectiveness across various settings where it might normally be implemented.

I. The Top Tier initiative's Expert Panel has identified this intervention as *Near Top Tier*

The Panel finds that this intervention meets the "Near Top Tier" evidence standard, defined as: Interventions shown to meet all elements of the Top Tier standard (i.e., well-conducted randomized controlled trials . . . showing sizable, sustained effects) in a single site, and which only need one additional step to qualify as Top Tier—a replication trial to confirm the initial findings and establish that they generalize to other sites.

II. Description of the Intervention

The Annual Book Fairs intervention provides students in high-poverty elementary schools with books to read over the summer, for three consecutive summers starting at the end of 1st or 2nd grade. The goal is to prevent summer learning loss—specifically, the well-established tendency for low-income children's reading achievement to fall relative to their more advantaged peers during the summer break. A number of studies have found that the loss is sizable, and may help explain the substantial and persistent reading achievement gap between more and less economically-advantaged students in the United States (e.g., Cooper et al., 1996; Alexander et al., 2007).

In the spring of each school year, students attend the fair, located in their school building, where they can order from among 400–600 books in a variety of genres (e.g., pop culture, series books, science). At each fair, students pick 12 books to keep as their own, which are delivered to them on the final day of school.

The study does not report the exact cost of the intervention, but indicates it was low—the main cost being that of supplying the students with 12 free books per year (which suggests a total 3-year cost of $175–$225 per student).

III. Evidence of Effectiveness

This summary of the evidence is based on a systematic search of the literature, and correspondence with leading researchers, to identify all well-conducted randomized controlled trials.

BOOK FAIR INTERVENTION. Our search identified one such trial. What follows is a summary of the study design and the program's effects on the main outcomes measured in the study, including any such outcomes for which no or adverse effects were found. All effects shown are statistically significant at the 0.05 level unless stated otherwise.

1. Our search identified one other randomized controlled trial of a book fair program, but we do not summarize the trial here because that program differed substantially from the intervention described above. For example, the book fair in that program was provided at the end of 4th grade (as opposed to 1st through 3rd grade) and one time only (as opposed to 3 consecutive years).

2. Specifically, the average annual gain in reading achievement for U.S. students during 4th and 5th grades on seven nationally normed tests is 0.36 and 0.40 standard deviations, respectively (see Bloom, Hill, Black, & Lipsey, 2008, referenced at the end of this summary). The difference in achievement between book fair and control group students, shown above, is 35–40% of these annual gains.

OVERVIEW OF THE STUDY DESIGN: RANDOMIZED CONTROLLED TRIAL OF THE ANNUAL BOOK FAIRS INTERVENTION IN 17 HIGH-POVERTY FLORIDA ELEMENTARY SCHOOLS. This was a randomized controlled trial of 1,713 1st- and 2nd-graders from 17 high-poverty elementary schools in two large school districts in Florida. Students were randomly assigned to (1) a group that received the Annual Book Fairs intervention, or (2) a control group that did not.

Approximately 89% of the students in the sample were either African American or Hispanic, and more than 65% were eligible for free or reduced-price lunch.

EFFECTS OF THE INTERVENTION APPROXIMATELY 3 YEARS AFTER RANDOM ASSIGNMENT (I.E., WHEN MOST STUDENTS WERE IN 4TH OR 5TH GRADE): Compared to the control group, students in the Book Fair group:

•   Scored higher on Florida's state-mandated test of reading achievement by 0.14 standard deviations, which equates to about 35–40% of a grade level.

•   Reported reading more often during their summer breaks (the effect size is unclear, because the study used an index of reading frequency that does not lend itself to ready interpretation).

Discussion of study quality

- The study had low-to-moderate sample attrition and a reasonably long-term follow-up: Outcome data from the state reading assessment were collected for 79% of the Book Fair group and 76% of the control group at the 3-year follow-up.

- The Book Fair and control group students in the 3-year follow-up sample were similar in their observable characteristics (i.e., demographics and pre-program reading ability).

- The study evaluated the Annual Book Fairs intervention as delivered in 17 high-poverty public schools, thus providing evidence of its effectiveness under real-world implementation conditions.

- The study measured outcomes using Florida's state-mandated reading assessment—the Florida Comprehensive Assessment Test (FCAT)—whose reliability and validity are well established. The test primarily measures passage and word comprehension.

- The study appropriately obtained parental consent for their children to participate in the study prior to random assignment.

- A limitation of this study is that students in the Book Fairs group were dropped from the study sample at the 3-year follow-up if they were no longer enrolled at one of the 17 schools conducting the Book Fairs (on the rationale that they probably did not receive the full intervention). By contrast, control group students were dropped only if they moved out of the school district entirely. This problem—an "intention-to-treat" violation—has the potential to undermine the equivalence of the Book Fairs and control groups. However, in this case, it appears to be at most a limited problem since students in the Book Fairs group who left their school often transferred to one of the other 17 schools providing the Book Fairs, and so were included in the final sample. As a result, the Book Fairs and control groups had similar rates of sample retention at the 3-year follow-up (79% and 76% respectively) and remained similar in observable pre-program characteristics, as noted above.

- A second study limitation is that its sample was geographically concentrated in two Florida school districts. The Top Tier initiative's Expert Panel believes that replication of the above findings in a second trial, conducted in another setting by the same or other researchers, would be desirable to confirm that the program is effective in other settings where it would normally be implemented.

IV. Summary of the Intervention's Benefits and Costs

If taxpayers fund implementation, what benefits to society can they expect to result, and what would be their net cost? The following provides a summary:

BENEFITS TO SOCIETY: An increase in students' reading achievement by 35–40% of a grade level, 3 years after random assignment.

NET COST TO TAXPAYERS. Cost was not explicitly reported, but consists mainly of supplying each student with 12 free books per year (which suggests a total 3-year cost of $175–$225 per student).

REFERENCES

Alexander, K. L., Entwisle, D. R., & Olson, L. S. (2007). Lasting consequences of the summer learning gap. *American Sociological Review, 72*(2), 167–180.

Bloom, H. S., Hill, C., Rebeck Black, A., & Lipsey, M. (2008). *Performance trajectories and performance gaps as achievement effect-size benchmarks for educational interventions.* MDRC Working Paper on Research Methodology.

Cooper, H., Nye, B., Charlton, K., Lindsay, J., & Greathouse, S. (1996). The effects of summer vacation on achievement test scores: A narrative and meta-analytic review. *Review of Educational Research, 66*(3, Fall), 227–268.

About the Contributors

Richard L. Allington is professor of literacy studies at the University of Tennessee in Knoxville. He is an accomplished scholar with over 150 published papers and ten books. His research has been funded by the U.S. Office of Educational Research and Improvement and the National Institutes of Health. He is the past president of both the International Reading Association and the Literacy Research Association. Twice he has been recipient of the Albert J. Harris Award from the Intentional Reading Association, most recently in 2012 for his research with Anne McGill-Franzen on addressing summer reading loss effectively with the distribution of self-selected books for summer reading to children from low-income families.

Lynn Bigelman has been an educator for over 20 years. She has been a classroom teacher, a reading specialist and, for the past 12 years, an elementary school principal. She has served as the president of the Michigan Reading Association as well as the president of Oakland County Reading Council. Lynn loves working and learning with her award-winning staff. She serves on various committees including the International Reading Association's Classroom and Teacher Awards Committee.

James J. Lindsay is a senior researcher with the American Institutes for Research. Much of Dr. Lindsay's work involves producing comprehensive summaries of research on particular topics using a set of statistical procedures called meta-analysis. He also is a certified reviewer for the What Works Clearinghouse, a trusted source for determining whether research evidence supports educational interventions. Dr. Lindsay has co-authored book chapters on meta-analysis and has conducted meta-analytic research reviews on the subjects of children's loss of academic skills over the summer, the behavioral cues to deception, and the impact of book distribution programs on children's outcomes (a review commissioned by Reading Is Fundamental).

Anne McGill-Franzen is professor of literacy studies and director of the Reading Center at the University of Tennessee. In addition to twice receiving the Albert J. Harris Award for research contributing to our understanding of reading/learning disabilities, Dr. McGill-Franzen has also received the Nila Banton Smith Research Dissemination Award and the Dina Feitelson Award from the International Reading Association for her work with emergent readers. She is the author of a number of published research reports and of several books, the most recent being the *Handbook of Reading Disabilities Research.* She has also been involved in the Diagnostic Teaching program co-sponosred by UNICEF and IRA in developing greater expertise in elementary school teachers in several African nations.

Geraldine Melosh began her career as an educator in Liberia, West Africa as a U.S. Peace Corps Volunteer where she taught high school English. In the 1980s she and her family moved to northeast Florida, where she became the elected superintendent of schools. While working on her doctorate at the University of Florida, Melosh founded The Children's Reading Center, Inc., a Florida literacy nonprofit and charter school for which she serves as principal. For 4 of the last 5 years, this elementary school has earned the distinction of being a Florida "A" school. In 2009, Melosh returned to Liberia to conduct staff development in reading with primary teachers in a new literacy endeavor called Liberia Reads! To date, she and a team of Liberian educators have trained over 70 Liberian teachers and principals in the basic skills to teach reading to over 2,500 primary grade students.

Lunetta Williams is an associate professor of literacy education at the University of North Florida. She received her doctoral degree from the University of Florida and while there worked as a research assistant on the *Summer Books!* Project. Dr. Williams's work focuses on minimizing the reading achievement gap between economically disadvantaged and advantaged children.

Index